EDI
IRVI

As part of our ongoing market research, we are always pleased to receive comments about our books, suggestions for new titles, or requests for catalogues. Please write to: The Editorial Director, Patrick Stephens Limited, Sparkford, Nr Yeovil, Somerset BA22 7JJ.

EDDIE
IRVINE

THE LUCK OF THE IRISH

Adam Cooper

Patrick Stephens Limited

'To absent friends: Roland and Jeff'

First published in 1996

British Library Cataloguing-in-Publication Data:
A catalogue record for this book is
available from the British Library

ISBN: 1 85260 560 X

Library of Congress catalog card no. 96 75826

Patrick Stephens Limited is an imprint of Haynes Publishing,
Sparkford, Nr Yeovil, Somerset BA22 7JJ.

Designed and typeset by G&M, Raunds, Northamptonshire
Printed and bound in Great Britain by
WBC, Bridgend, Mid Glam.

Contents

Acknowledgements

THIS BOOK WAS never intended to be Eddie Irvine's own version of events, and in any case his memories of the early days are particularly vague! However, snatches of interviews I've done with him over the years appear throughout the text. Eddie tends to leave his mark on people, and the story is instead shaped by the recollections of dozens of folk who have worked with him or raced against him.

Although I did not have enough space to quote all of them, I would like to thank the following for their help: Kenny Acheson, Marco Apicella, Rubens Barrichello, Dick Bennetts, Martin Brundle, Gustav Brunner, Graham Bogle, Martin Donnelly, Mike Earle, Bernie Ecclestone, Eje Elgh, Ralph Firman, Trevor Foster, Heinz-Harald Frentzen, Mark Gallagher, Andrew Gilbert-Scott, Brian Hart, Damon Hill, Clifton Hughes, Alan Jenkins, Eddie Jordan, Tom Kristensen, Nick Langley, JJ Lehto, David Marren, Richard Martin, Mauro Martini, Allan McNish, Alain Menu, Luca di Montezemolo, Yuichi Murayama, Emanuele Naspetti, Steve Nichols, Malcolm Oastler, Stephen Patton, Richard Peacock, Ian Phillips, Malcolm 'Puddy' Pullen, Michael Schumacher, Martin Spence, Mike Thompson, Jean Todt, John Uprichard, Jacques Villeneuve, John Watson, Tim Wright, Keith Wiggins, Richard Young and especially the Irvine family, Ed, Kathleen and Sonia.

Help with sourcing pictures was provided by Autosport Photographic, John Townsend (Formula One Pictures), Jad Sherif (Pan Images), John Dunbar (Zooom Photographic), Stephanie de Kantzow (PR Plus), Empics, Spectator Newspapers, Tom Hicks and Ian Lynas. Thanks are due to *Autosport* for permission to reproduce the odd quote. I would also like to acknowledge Brendan Lynch's splendid book *Green Dust: Ireland's Unique*

Motor Racing History 1900–1939 (Portobello, 1988), which tells the full story of the Ards TT. Inspiration for the chapter titles was provided by some of Eddie's favourite Irish musicians, including his mate Van Morrison, who recently bought the house next door to his! This project wouldn't have reached fruition without the support of Tinneke Geenen, my parents, and the good folk at Haynes (Darryl Reach, Alison Roelich and Flora Myer), and I would like to thank all of them for their endless patience.

Finally, I would like to dedicate this book to the memory of Roland Ratzenberger and Jeff Krosnoff, two men who helped me enormously when I covered racing in Japan in 1992–3, and with whom Eddie and I shared many an enjoyable night in Tokyo. I told Jeff of my plans early in 1996, but sadly never had the chance to chase him for Irvine anecdotes, or the candid snapshots he'd promised to send. He had some good stories to tell . . .

Straight from the grid

BRANDS HATCH, 18 JULY 1976. It's the middle of the hottest summer in years, and the spectator banks are packed with sun-burned enthusiasts. Most are at the British Grand Prix for one reason: they want to see James Hunt, darling of the hour, defeat the Ferraris.

Somewhere in the 75,000-strong crowd, 10-year-old Eddie Irvine sits on the parched grass with his Dad, Mum and sister Sonia, keen racing fans all. As usual they've come all the way to Kent from their home in Northern Ireland for a week's holiday. The resourceful Irvine kids have been busy chasing the famous, and they clutch a programme autographed by Hunt himself, as well as John Watson, Mario Andretti, Jody Scheckter, Jochen Mass, Vittorio Brambilla, Stirling Moss and Ken Tyrrell. They've even managed to nab a genuine pop star; one of the pages bears the legend, 'To Edmund — best wishes mate, Alvin Stardust'. When the action gets under way, Hunt makes sure the trip is really worth it.

The race starts amid chaos. Dust and debris fly as the Ferraris of Niki Lauda and Clay Regazzoni tangle at the first corner, and Hunt's McLaren can't avoid them. He tips up onto two wheels, slams back down, and carries on at the tail of the field, his steering bent. The race is stopped, and a little later officials announce that Hunt, his car still in tatters, won't be allowed to take the re-start in the spare. The crowd doesn't like the sound of that, and thousands of angry voices, including the Irvines', have their say. By now, sneaking round the pits on his own with nothing resembling a proper pass, Eddie watches the arguments with interest.

During a lengthy delay the McLaren team manages to fix Hunt's car, and he's safely back in place on the grid for the second attempt. Lauda's Ferrari leads, as it has done at so many races in the past couple of seasons. But this

Ferrari advisor Niki Lauda and Eddie chat in 1996. Eddie used to be close to Lauda's great friend and rival, James Hunt. (Pan Images)

time, the Austrian can't hold off Hunt, and the Englishman sweeps past and goes on to score a memorable win. The cheers echo around Brands, and like everyone else, young Eddie has got the result he wanted — Ferrari beaten by Hunt, fair and square. And just to make the family's day complete, their other favourite driver, fellow Ulsterman Watson, finishes fourth. They head back to the campsite in happy mood, unaware that Hunt will later be disqualified.

MELBOURNE, 9 MARCH 1996. Just a few minutes remain of the single qualifying session for the Australian GP, first race of the new season. Against expectations, newcomer Jacques Villeneuve has pipped Williams team-mate Damon Hill to pole position, while World Champion Michael Schumacher has hauled the troublesome and virtually untested Ferrari F310 into third place.

The cars file back into the Albert Park pit lane as the drivers complete their allotted 12 laps and the hour runs out. A few are still circulating, so the positions on the TAG/Heuer timing screen are not quite set in stone. Suddenly, there's a change. The hitherto unbeatable Schumacher is bounced out of the top three, not by a rival Benetton or McLaren, but by his own team-mate — Eddie Irvine.

The Australian fans raise a cheer at this surprise news. In the Ferrari pits, team advisor Niki Lauda allows himself a wry smile, while in the Eurosport commentary box John Watson goes into overdrive at his young country-man's performance. The next day Schumacher soon passes Eddie but retires with brake failure, and Irvine brings his Ferrari safely home in third place behind the flying Williams duo. After the race Eddie gives his proud Dad the perfect birthday present — the crash helmet he wore in his first Grand Prix for Ferrari.

In the 20 years that separate those two episodes, the lad from Newtownards moved from wide-eyed spectator to driver for the most famous and charismatic team in Grand Prix racing. He managed it thanks to a combination of talent, a happy knack for making his own luck, and a gift for winning people over with his honesty and ever present grin.

One of the many who helped him along the way was James Hunt. The former World Champion died a few months before Eddie gatecrashed the F1 scene in 1993, but his support came a few years earlier, at a crucial stage of his former fan's career. Even people unaware of this past connection make comparisons between the two men. At a time when most Grand Prix drivers appear to be single-purpose clones Irvine seems to hark back to a bygone era, when drivers were colourful characters with time for things other than just racing cars. And there's more to it than a shared interest in fast cars and the opposite sex:

'There were a lot of similarities, despite them coming from different ends of the social scale,' says Ian Phillips, commercial director of Jordan GP and former journalist. 'There were always things happening when they were around! Also, James, when he got into F1, had a shocking reputation; Hunt the Shunt and all the rest of it. Eddie was very much the same. Because he'd been in Japan for three years, nobody knew who he was. He arrived at Suzuka in '93, created a storm, and said what he said in his very open way. It was just like James. People just didn't know how to take him, just as they didn't know how to take James.

'But they both had the intelligence to work the situation out, to get themselves in a position where they could deliver, surround themselves with people who believed the same as they did, and actually make it happen for themselves. Eddie's got it all worked out, have no fear, just in the same way that James did.'

From scrap dealer's son, having a bit of fun in an old Formula Ford at the local track, to Ferrari Grand Prix driver — he may easily be dismissed by some as a non-conforming wild man, but there's much more to Eddie Irvine than meets the eye. That's what this story is about.

• CHAPTER ONE •

Do anything you wanna do

NEWTOWNARDS IS A sleepy little place. Situated 12 miles east of Belfast, this small collection of pubs and shops has for the most part avoided the Irish troubles. It doesn't give the appearance of having a role in motorsport history, yet the Ulster town's Conway Square was once as familiar to the top racers as Casino Square, a world away in Monte Carlo.

Each autumn from 1928 to 1936, the streets were blocked off to form part of the 13.6-mile course for the Ards Tourist Trophy, reckoned by some to be the biggest sporting event of the day in the British Isles. The cars roared into Newtownards from the direction of Dundonald, where the pits and startline were located, and charged under the railway bridge into Regent St. They would make a hard right into Conway Square, before leaving on South St and heading to nearby Comber, and back to Dundonald.

The TT was a massive event attracting huge crowds. All the greats of the pre-war years took part. German ace Rudolf Caracciola triumphed for Mercedes in 1929, and others to appear included Dick Seaman, Bentley boys Tim Birkin and Lord Howe, Prince B Bira, Louis Chiron, record-breaker John Cobb, and the enigmatic William Grover-Williams, winner of the first Monaco GP. The legendary Tazio Nuvolari won twice, the first time in 1930 when he led Giuseppe Campari and Achille Varzi in a 1–2–3 for the unbeatable Alfa Romeo team. A year later Baconin Borzacchini replaced Varzi, and salvaged second after team-mates Nuvolari and Campari hit mechanical problems.

Like so many other classic road races, the Ards TT was brought to a premature end by a tragedy. In the 1936 event, blighted by heavy rain, Jack Chambers crashed his Riley entering Newtownards, near the railway bridge. Eight spectators were killed, and the event was not run again. While the

TT later found a post-war home at Dundrod, to the north west of Belfast, Newtownards became just a footnote in Ireland's colourful racing history.

Eddie Irvine grew up in and around Regent St, Conway Square and South St. He had only a vague idea that the roads where he first kicked a football and rode his bicycle had such a glorious past. Yet there is a direct path from Eddie to those famous chargers. The pre-war visitors included an ambitious Italian who'd retired from driving to take up team management, and who in 1930 and 1931 oversaw the works Alfas of Nuvolari and company in the Ards TT. Sixty-four years to the month after the great Enzo Ferrari last visited County Down, the Formula 1 team that bears his name hired Eddie Irvine. Furthermore, Eddie's paternal grandfather, Harry Irvine, watched the race and would have seen Ferrari's Alfa team in action. Although he didn't drive at the time, he took a keen interest as some of the teams were based in a garage near his workplace, and he would look around the cars and talk to the drivers.

Harry Irvine and his wife Ena had seven children, four sons and three daughters, the youngest of whom was Edmund, born in March 1941. Known to most as Ed, he worked as an apprentice plasterer, and later got a job as a hodsman, carrying bricks for bricklayers. After that he spent two years in a hosiery factory.

There were few job opportunities to be had locally at that time, and many Ulster folk looked abroad. Ed's three brothers and one of his sisters went to Canada. In 1959, aged 18, Ed followed them to Toronto. Out there

The Ards TT course went straight through the centre of Newtownards.

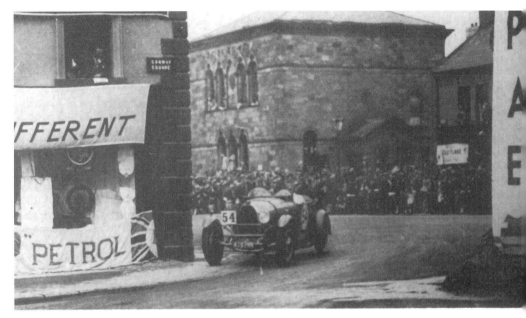

Bugatti's Albert Divo negotiates Conway Square.

he developed an interest in motor racing, encouraged by brothers Jimmy and Tommy. They soon discovered Westwood, the nearest track to Toronto, and in 1961 the threesome saw Stirling Moss win the first big sportscar event at the newly opened Mosport Park. The enterprising Irvines gate-crashed the podium celebrations, and Ed patted his hero Moss on the back — he claims he didn't wash his hand after that for months! A photo of the great moment appeared in the following year's programme.

The Irvines also went to Watkins Glen, just over the border, to see Innes Ireland head home Dan Gurney and Tony Brooks in the 1961 US GP. They had no qualms about introducing themselves to the stars in the relaxed paddocks of the day, and Ed chatted with the likes of Moss, Ireland and Jim Clark.

After three years in Canada, Ed decided to head back home. He had a very good reason. Just a week before he first left Bangor he'd met Kathleen McGowan. One of five children, her father — like Ed's, an orphan — was the popular caretaker at Regent House School in Newtownards, while her mother ran a couple of shops in the town. Kathleen didn't fancy shop life, and worked in a garment factory.

Apart from a brief trip back one Christmas, Ed hadn't see her during his absence, but they'd kept in touch by letter. The year after his return they were married. At first the young couple lived with Ed's parents as they couldn't afford a home of their own — he had blown most of his savings buying an MGA sportscar. They later moved into a house in South St, right on the old TT course. Daughter Sonia was born on 18 April 1964, and a son followed on 10 November 1965.

Ed wanted to call the boy Stirling Moss Irvine, but Kathleen didn't approve. They finally settled on plain Edmund. There was no middle name, creating confusion among everyone who came across the family in years to come. To make things easier, I'll continue to call the father Ed and the son Eddie.

On his return from Canada Ed had gone back to his job in the hosiery factory, but he also started to make money in his spare time by buying insurance write-offs and stripping them for spare parts. The business grew and his father, having retired from his job at Bangor nursery, looked after it during the day, while Ed worked at the factory. Brother Jimmy, who returned from Canada a couple of years later, also got involved.

Inspired by what they'd seen at Mosport Park and Watkins Glen, Jimmy and Ed took an interest in events at nearby Kirkistown, just 15 miles south

Edmund Irvine Sr with daughter Sonia in 1996. He sparked Eddie's racing interest. (Formula One Pictures)

Brotherly love. Eddie and Sonia were close in their youth and she works for him today as his physio. (Formula One Pictures)

of Newtownards. They both had a desire to try racing. The first step was to trade Ed's MGA and a Triumph TR3 Jimmy had brought back from Canada for a Lotus 18 Formula Junior, the early 1960s equivalent of Formula Ford. The plan was for them to share the car, but Jimmy's wife didn't approve. He became the mechanic while Ed took care of the driving.

'Ed was a bit of a man of mystery when he arrived,' says journalist, competitor and now Kirkistown manager Richard Young, 'Northern Ireland being the kind of place where if people don't know your grandad intimately they'd look at you with great suspicion! The family had no motor racing pedigree and had a scrapyard, and were therefore rather sniffed at by some of the establishment of the time.'

Ulster had two race circuits. There was also Bishopscourt, a little further away in County Down. Early 1968 saw the opening of a third venue, Mondello Park, south of the border in Eire.

Racing became a family outing for the Irvines, and young Sonia and Eddie came along for the ride. It was a bit of fun at the weekends. Few of the Irish drivers had serious ambitions to race internationally. One who did however was bearded Belfast youngster John Watson: his last days in Irish racing coincided with Ed's first steps.

After the Lotus, Ed and Jimmy wheeled and dealed their way through a series of F3 Brabhams, and at one time used an engine which had belonged to the Brazilian Carlos Pace, a Formula 1 star of the future. Ed raced mainly in the Club Specials category, for 1-litre powered single-seaters. His nemesis was Wilson Nicholl, who always seemed to leave Ed in the bridesmaid role. This was the *Autosport* report of 27 August 1970:

'For once it looked as if the perennial Lotus 18 of Wilson Nicholl was going to be given a run for its money as the Brabham of Ed Irvine sat on its tail for three laps. Then suddenly the Brabham fell back with gear selection troubles and the Lotus went on to its customary win.'

In 1971 Ed had a new rival, as reported on 10 June: 'Roy Courtney took the lead in his immaculate Crossle 17F and looked like winning easily. However Edmund Irvine got his Brabham within range and for the remainder of the race the pair fought it out.'

A week later at Bishopscourt Ed nearly had his revenge, when Courtney 'was phenomenally slow on the corners but much quicker than challenger Edmund Irvine's Brabham on the straights. In his frantic efforts to get in front Irvine spun at Perrie on the last lap.'

Finally, in September 1971 he had a chance to beat Courtney at Kirkistown, when '. . . gradually Ed Irvine's Brabham reduced the leeway to take the lead on the last lap and win by a second'.

Young Eddie, not quite six, must have been a proud lad that day, for as far as anyone can recall this was his Dad's only race win. Just once, in July 1972, did Ed venture over to a mainland circuit, joining up with a fellow racer and taking in Formula Libre races at Croft, just outside York, and Ingliston, in Edinburgh. The trip was not a success. At Croft, Ed was hauled off the grid when marshals mistakenly thought his car was leaking oil, although he was later allowed out in another race. In Scotland he waited in vain for the Union Jack with which races were started in those days. Eventually someone waved a strange blue flag with a white cross, and the surprised Ed was left sitting as he watched the locals take off! Afterwards the truck broke down just outside Edinburgh, and the party of six spent three days sleeping in a service area before they could get going once again.

Ed's last racing car was an ex-works F3 Chevron B17C. Then in 1973 he decided to hang up his helmet in order to concentrate on business and bringing up the kids. The Chevron was sold, and the proceeds spent on carpeting the house. However, motor racing remained a family interest. Every year they would pack the camping gear and head to Brands Hatch or Silverstone and take in the British Grand Prix. Sonia and Eddie would hang around at the helicopter pad in order to grab autographs from the

Right *School days at Kirkistown. Teacher Richard Peacock crouches by the side of a Crossle 32F. Eddie displays his nice line in jumpers.* (Spectator Newspapers)

Ready to go! Eddie with the Crossle 50F he acquired at the start of his first season of racing. (Spectator Newspapers)

arriving drivers — Watson and James Hunt being among their favourites. After the race the family would stay on for a few days, and the camper would occasionally go home with extra luggage in the form of John Player Special banners, pot plants, plastic chains and other ephemera carelessly left around the hospitality areas, and which the Irvines assumed had been abandoned.

Meanwhile, the scrap business was expanding. Ed and his father now worked full-time in recovering damaged cars from all over Ireland, repairing and selling them.

Sonia and Eddie were close as they grew up. Eddie was a determined child, prone to getting what he wanted at any cost, and able to come up smiling whatever the punishment inflicted by his mum. Kathleen was always keen for the kids to get involved in sport, and entered them both in an annual bicycle race around Newtownards. Family memories are contradictory but Eddie, relishing his first ever competitive outing on wheels, recalls that he won. Later, both children took up swimming. What Eddie lacked in technique he made up for in vigour, and his 'flailing windmill' style earned him a prize for effort in his very first race.

He soon improved. He and Sonia joined the swimming club and started training properly, which meant Dad had to get them up and drag them over to the local pool for the 7–8am session, before they headed off to Castle Gardens Primary School. Not too keen on waking up, they sometimes slept outside in the family motor caravan to avoid having to rise a moment earlier than necessary. Eddie was smaller than most of his rivals, but he was good at both the backstroke and breaststroke. At one time he was ranked second in Ulster and sixth in all-Ireland.

But Eddie always hated training. His interest in swimming waned after he broke his leg when roller skating, aged 15. Not that the family took too much notice of a mere plaster. One day when Eddie criticised his Mum's driving she promptly stopped the car a couple of miles from home, and invited him to get out and walk the rest of the journey. Only later did she remember that he was incapacitated. He made it home covered in mud having crawled across the fields.

At Regent House School Eddie was smart but lazy. He still managed to sail through his O-levels however, taking a particular interest in physics, but he couldn't be persuaded to stay on for A-levels, instead planning to join his father in the family business. Ed didn't want that though. He insisted that his son sign on the dole — on the proviso that he told them he was looking for a job, but didn't want any unemployment money. The theory was that this would teach young Eddie the value of working for a living. But he returned from the DHSS office with a glum face — the staff had apparently thought that he was from a wealthy family and had no business wasting their time. Eddie's next step was a business course at Bangor Technical College, but his heart was no longer in studying and he didn't stick at it for long. So Ed relented, and gave him a job.

Eddie gained his first experience of driving in his Dad's old scrap cars, sometimes on a nearby construction site, and sometimes, when no-one was around, on the streets. Before he passed his test he acquired a rather unusual road car, as family friend Stephen Patton explains:

'He bought a Lotus Elan with a V4 Ford Transit van engine in it. It was lethal and you could have got killed in it very easily, because the engine was too heavy! He was very into sportscars. I got a Ferrari Dino for next to nothing, and it really was a tool. I called round and offered him a run, and I think it would have been the first time he was ever in a Ferrari. He was just so impressed with it, compared to the sort of things we usually had. He always said to me, "I'm going to get myself a Ferrari. I don't know why anybody buys a Porsche!"'

Eddie also had fun riding an old motocross bike in the local fields. When he asked for a bike for the road, Ed thought it too dangerous. Instead, he suggested that the lad might like to have a go in a racing car, which would give him something to channel his energy into. Some 10 years had passed since Ed last competed, and the idea was that he'd race and Eddie would be allowed to have the odd run round. The teenager didn't have to be asked twice.

They found a Crossle 32F which had been raced by the son of a Belfast car dealer, and Ed duly part-exchanged an old Ford Capri which he'd recently done up. Built just down the road from the Irvine home by veteran constructor John Crossle, the 32F was not a new car, but it had been a classic of its type. Just five years earlier Nigel Mansell raced one in the British FF1600 series.

Ed had one comeback race in the Crossle at Kirkistown in March 1982. The day was spoiled when he had an off in practice, and Kathleen had to persuade him to fork out £150 for a new radiator so he could take the start. He enjoyed the outing, but perhaps not as much as he'd expected to. Aged 41 he decided that young Eddie would probably get more pleasure from the car.

So it was that on a quiet weekday in 1982 16-year-old Eddie Irvine squeezed himself aboard his dad's racing car, and set off from the pitlane for a few exploratory laps of Kirkistown. The featureless 1.5-mile course is not the most challenging of circuits. It's basically triangular in shape, with a couple of fast kinks in two of the straights, and a chicane in the other. Debtors Dip, Colonial One and Two, Fisherman's Bend and the Hairpin would become familiar to Eddie over the next couple of years. But on this day it was all new. He remembers 'spinning like a top all over the place,' but when he came back to the pits he was grinning.

'I can still see the look on his face,' Ed recalls. 'I'd never seen him so excited about anything before.'

Father and son came to a simple agreement. Eddie would work for the family business, but he wouldn't be paid; anything he earned would go into his racing. He accepted with enthusiasm, and worked seven days a week. His duties included crushing old car bodies with a huge metal weight and lifting them onto a truck before they were taken off to a Belfast scrapyard.

As a sideline, the Irvines briefly got into the fruit and veg business, exporting potatoes to England. After he passed his driving test, Eddie would go round the countryside in a Morris Minor Traveller, picking up samples.

Edmund Irvine Sr, the man whose enthusiasm led his son to Ferrari. (Author)

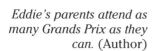

Eddie's parents attend as many Grands Prix as they can. (Author)

21

On the way home, with the extra ballast in the back, he would slide the car around and have a bit of fun. One merchant in Birmingham paid good money, but when he bounced a cheque for £5,000 the Irvines realised why his prices seemed so fair. They never recovered the cash, and that was the end of the potato business.

Eddie continued with his informal testing at Kirkistown. Englishman Richard Peacock, who runs the circuit's racing school, was an early fan:

'They asked if they could come and join in with the racing school and do a bit of testing. It was a weekday and it was reasonably quiet, so that was fine. They were doing their own thing and I wandered over to see them. The tyres they had on the car, I can remember even now; I wouldn't have used them as fenders on a ferry! They were horrendous. They said they were saving the good ones, and I told them to put some decent rubber on it and it would go a bit better. Which they duly did, and I think lap times improved by about three seconds a lap. It was a very logical thing to do to put some old tyres on to practice, but they were that old and that horrible that he wasn't going to learn anything!

'This arrangement continued, with them coming down practising, and then one day, Eddie Sr came over and said, "look, can I book him into the school, he won't bloody well listen to me — perhaps he'll listen to you!" Which of course is always the case; people react differently to parents. So young Eddie came to the school and was a very competent pupil, although I'm afraid I couldn't turn round then and say he was going to make it. There is so much learning to do, you don't say "he's going to be a Grand Prix star one day". But he obviously always had talent.

'One of the things about Eddie is that he's refreshing, and was so refreshing even then, because he loves life. He really is good fun to be with. The average modern racing driver is such a pain in the arse. They take themselves so seriously. And Eddie never has. He's always just wanted to go racing and could probably teach many young drivers a thing or two.'

It was soon apparent that the 32F wasn't really up to the job, and the Irvines traded up to a more modern but still second-hand 50F. Painted a sinister black, this was a good-looking car, but it was not the best Crossle design and had a reputation for being a difficult beast.

'If they'd asked me I would probably have told them not to do that,' says Peacock, 'because it probably wasn't a step in the right direction. He didn't really do as well as he should have done in that. He would have done better sticking with the 32F.'

Still, by the start of 1983 Eddie Irvine was ready to go racing.

• CHAPTER TWO •

Teenage kicks

AT THE TIME Eddie Irvine started his racing career, Ulster had no fewer than three drivers at the very top of the sport, and their success must have been an inspiration to the lad. McLaren star John Watson had come close to winning the 1982 World Championship, and Tommy Byrne had shown that the impossible could be achieved by making it from Kirkistown to Grand Prix racing on talent alone. However, his GP drives with the Theodore team at the end of 1982 ultimately led nowhere, and when Kenny Acheson reached F1 with the RAM team in late 1983 he too didn't stay long.

Eddie's first race outings, at Kirkistown in March 1983, were unspectacular. Only 17 he was often up against experienced drivers, some of whom, like veteran Tommy Reid, had been racing at Kirkistown since the Watson days. The second-hand tyres and awkward Crossle chassis did not help, but it was all part of his education. There were a couple of sixth places and then, in September, a third, albeit after several cars ahead had fallen off. Later outings in big events at Phoenix and Mondello, south of the border, were more impressive.

Friend Stephen Patton, who worked for Crossle, recalls the early days: 'I always remember that he just seemed to enjoy himself, it was all great fun. The motor racing, at that time, was the greatest thing he'd ever done. He was really enthusiastic, probably more enthusiastic than the average young fella. When you look back on it you suddenly realise the amount of commitment he had, compared to a lot of young lads'.

Eddie did little to attract attention in his first season, and the man who earned all the plaudits was Belfast's Martin Donnelly. Nineteen months older, he had a big sponsor and swept up in the FF2000 category. One man who did notice Eddie was sometime racer Clifton Hughes, who became an early mentor.

SUCCESSFUL DEBUT FOR CONLIG DRIVER

"Spectator", Thursday, 3rd November.

While all the hustle and bustle of Formula One racing continues with talk of £1 million plus contracts in the offing, a 17-year-old Conlig driver is quietly saving his money to keep his Formula Ford racer on the local racing circuit next season after his successful debut this year.

Young Edmund Irvine has taken his 1982 Crosslé 50F to a number of meetings at Kirkistown and Mondello this season and has turned in some admirable performances which should give the more experienced drivers something to worry about.

Many drivers can say they took part in 20 races this season but Edmund is probably one of the few who can say he started and finished all his 20 races. This is even more to his credit when you consider that Formula Ford racing at Kirkistown can be extremely hairy at times and you have to be both good and lucky to stay out of trouble.

It was not just a matter of starting and finishing these races though. Probably the youngest driver at Kirkistown, Edmund recorded two wins, a third, and a fifth and sixth place during his season's racing against the best drivers in the Province and quite a few from Dublin who made the journey.

At Phoenix Park this year his sixth place in a Formula Ford heat qualified him for the final where he came 11th from the total of 55 cars taking part.

Perhaps his best achievement came at Mondello during the Formula Ford Festival race. With 40 cars taking part Edmund recorded a fine fourth place in his heat and an encouraging fifth place in the final against drivres with an awful lot more experience of racing and of that rack in particular.

Edmund's sleek black Crosslé has certainly proved to be a match for his talents. The first time he got into it was the night before a race meeting.

He attributes his good record to a period of lessons with the Richard Peacock school of racing and he is probably one of the school's best advertisements in Northern Ireland.

Edmund, who not surprisingly works with cars at his father's business at Green Road, Conlig, took a number of lessons under Richard Peacock and these gave him the proper training, theory and build up to a season's racing.

Up to now Edmund has been fortunate to be 'sponsored' largely by his father, who has himself been involved in racing for quite a while. The elder Edmund explained that his son put all his money into the car and this meant considerable restrictions socially on this non-smoking, tee-total youngster.

Now, however, with last season's total costs for racing totalling several thousand pounds, Edmund is on the lookout for a sponsor or someone who can help him with his future racing programme.

With such a promising career ahead of him in motorsport and the advantage of starting young, hopefully it will not be too difficult for Edmund to keep himself to the fore in future seasons.

Eddie's local paper recounts his 1983 season. Nobody can recall two proper wins and it's assumed they were in Formula Libre's FF1600 class . . . (The Spectator)

'At 17, he was really a little bit shy,' says Hughes. 'He was a very nice guy, laughing and smiling a lot, but he seemed almost to be a little bit introverted at the time. He was a teenager who didn't really appreciate what he was going to be capable of in the future. He was fairly modest about his abilities, very wet behind the ears as a racing driver.

'I do remember the first time I met him, I went down to the garage, and he took me for a drive in an old brown MGB his Dad had. It was a nice sunny day, and there were two revelations. The first was that he didn't try to drive the car particularly quickly, but he drove incredibly smoothly for a young man with so little experience. The other was that the place he was heading for was the seaside, where all the dolly birds were lying about on the beach. That hasn't changed one bit!'

With the short Kirkistown season over, in November the Irvines headed to England to spectate at the Brands Hatch Formula Ford Festival, where many of the Irish regulars were competing. This was a major event on the calendar, and an essential stepping stone for any youngster trying to work his way through the ranks. Around 150 drivers from all over the world would be whittled down through two days of heats, quarter finals and semis to the grand final. Just making the last 26 was an achievement. This was a big, big step from humble Kirkistown, and the Irvines knew that Eddie wasn't quite ready for it, but he learned a lot from just watching.

The big news that autumn was the birth of a new racing car manufacturer in Bangor, just a mile from the Irvine home. Crossle designer Leslie Drysdale left after 19 years to set up Mondiale, in conjunction with wealthy drivers Colin Lees and Dennis McGall. The Mondiale/Crossle rivalry would add a little spice to the 1984 season. Eddie started his second year in his trusty Crossle 50F, improved by a new set of shocks, but in the season opener at Kirkistown on 31 March he managed to collide with McGall's new Mondiale. His form soon improved, and he came fifth when he ventured down south to Mondello Park.

In May, several English drivers came over to Kirkistown for a round of the EFDA (European Formula Drivers Association) series, a sort of quasi-European championship with rounds in different regions across the continent. Dave Coyne, driving the works Duckhams-sponsored Van Diemen won both the regular local race and the later EFDA event, while Eddie took a fourth and a seventh. He was gradually becoming more competitive, but racing was all still just a bit of fun: 'At no stage did I think I was going to be a professional driver. I don't know what I was thinking at the time! There was no way it was going to happen anyway, as we had no money at all'.

In the summer, the Irvines took advantage of the local chassis wars and bought a new Mondiale M84S for a special price. First time out at Mondello Eddie had a couple of second places, and one of them was in another EFDA round where he was a surprise pole winner. Shortly after that he took part in a round of the RAC British Hillclimb Championship at nearby Craigantlet, and duly won the FF1600 class and set a new record — a unique statistic for a current Grand Prix driver!

Results in the EFDA races qualified Eddie to take part in the finale at Zandvoort on 16 September. He'd not yet raced outside Ireland, but the trip to Holland sounded attractive. He picked up a little sponsorship, and someone gave him a pair of racing boots — until then he'd driven in trainers. Ed welded a tow bar onto the back of his camper, found a proper trailer, and the whole entourage piled aboard and took the Belfast–Stranraer ferry.

First stop was Newcastle where Sonia was studying physiotherapy, and then they headed south and got the ferry to Hook of Holland, happily filling in a 'Nothing to Declare' form at the other end. In their innocence the Irvines hadn't realised that a racing car on a trailer might involve a little extra paperwork. The Dutch customs demanded a £1,000 deposit — about four times the cash they had with them. After a long delay and much telephoning it was sorted out with a generous loan from the Zandvoort circuit manager, and they finally arrived.

This was the first time the Irvines had come across the sort of strong, international field they'd observed at the Brands Festival. Coyne was there again, along with continental aces such as Harald Huysman, Eric Bachelart, Frank Biela and Gerrit Van Kouwen. Most drivers had impressive transporters, spare engines and the budgets to match. The Irvines learned the hard way. A rival team agreed to give them advice on gear ratios, and as the qualifying session drew near, they still hadn't come up with the vital information. Ed was waiting patiently with the gearbox in bits until it finally became apparent that they'd been sold a dummy. When Eddie did get out on the track, his engine was left gasping on the circuit's long straight. Nevertheless, he eventually finished 11th, and for the first time, Ed realised that perhaps his son really had something. Stephen Patton, who'd gone to help a top Scottish driver and ended up giving the Irvines a hand, was impressed.

'I reckon that race was when Eddie decided, "this is what I want to do". He went very, very well. He got the best possible result he could have got. I think he realised that racing at home was good experience, but he had to get himself over to England.'

Clifton Hughes agrees: 'He came back from that race full of enthusiasm. He said to me, "down the straights, the other guys were disappearing, but round the corners none of them were quicker than me". All of a sudden, he started to realise he could actually do it'.

When the group got back to Bangor, Mondiale checked the recently rebuilt engine and confirmed it wasn't running properly. Nevertheless, it had been a valuable experience, and for Eddie, Holland — and Amsterdam in particular — had been an eye opener.

'I can remember us going into the red light district,' recalls Patton. 'I think that was Eddie's introduction to all that.'

The next target was a first crack at the Formula Ford Festival at Brands in November. Eddie went over early to do some testing, which culminated in an entry in a Champion of Brands race — his debut in England. This was a fiercely fought contest, with rounds held every other week at the circuit's club meetings. As at Kirkistown several of the top drivers were older, self-made types who raced for fun. But the races were also a starting point for young guys. One particular newcomer, who'd already won a Brands title on bikes, had begun to go well. Like Eddie, Damon Hill had spent his youth following his dad round the race circuits, albeit in more glamorous locations. On 14 October Hill made the crucial step out of Graham's shadow when he scored his first ever four-wheeled win in a Champion of Brands race. Eddie joined the fray a fortnight later. Also in the field that day was another youngster who was starting to make a name for himself — Johnny Herbert. Eddie overcame a practice crash and here for the first time diced with future F1 rivals Hill and Herbert, until he lost time sliding wide at

The 1984 Brands Formula Ford Festival was the race that made Eddie's name. (Autosport)

A week after the Festival Eddie returned to Brands to score his first win. (Autosport)

Graham Hill Bend. His eventual seventh place was still respectable in the circumstances.

The Festival itself was a week later, and for Eddie it could hardly have gone better. In his heat on Saturday, he finished fourth, behind Tim Jones (son of Brian Jones, the Brands commentator), Pete Rogers and Bertrand Gachot, and three places ahead of Germany's Bernd Schneider. The big test came on Sunday, but he passed it with flying colours. In his quarter final he was third, and in the semi he managed fifth. He'd avoided all the shunts and made it to the final in his first Festival, which was no small achievement. With the two semis combined, the fifth place put him on the fourth row of the three-two-three-two grid for the final. Right alongside him was Damon Hill, also a Festival rookie.

He arrived as a total unknown and left as a man to watch

The race was shown on Grandstand, and thus marked Eddie's first appearance on national television — and the first time he'd been spotted by Murray Walker. The cameras captured a rather aggressive start by the youngster when he moved to the right and leaned on Hill as they approached Paddock Bend. Later, just as Murray made note of the fine job he was doing to head a line of cars, Eddie slid wide and Hill nipped through. Dutchman Van Kouwen won, ahead of Uwe Schafer, Gachot, Jonathan Bancroft, Hill, Pete Rogers and Eddie. He arrived as a total unknown, and left as a man to watch. In the small, close knit world of British Formula Ford, he'd made an impression on the right people.

'That was a brave old effort,' says Peacock. 'He hadn't had loads of testing, was under a lot of pressure the whole time, and drove very, very well. He had a queue of cars behind him and he kept his head.'

Suitably enthused, Eddie stayed on at Brands for the upcoming winter races, although he and mechanic cousin Stephen soon became bored with the four walls of the camper and the endless meals in the Kentagon bar at the top of the paddock. But the weekend race action made up for it. At the following week's Champion of Brands race, against all the experienced local drivers, Eddie won and set fastest lap — and earned the £50 Driver of the Day award. This was his first race victory. It came the day after his 19th birthday and just four weeks after Hill broke his own duck in the very same series. Confidence soared.

The following week Eddie took pole, but a rival complained and he wasn't allowed to start as he was only a reserve, having submitted his entry too late. In the final race of the season two weeks later he set fastest lap and finished second — ahead of Herbert — and picked up another Driver of the Day award.

Suddenly, racing was becoming serious. What had been a bit of fun for the young lad now showed signs of providing him with a future. His success had not gone unnoticed by Mondiale, and the company was keen for him to showcase its products in the British series in 1985. With the aid of a certain Eddie Jordan, a deal was put together for the youngster to drive a works-supported car prepared by Kiwi Murray Taylor, who usually concentrated on F3. This was a big break, but it wasn't free: the Irvines had to find £10,000 for the privilege of running with a professional team. 'It might as well have been £100,000 at that stage,' Ed noted later. Selling their own Mondiale raised around half of that, and Ed had to use his initiative to get the rest. He told a finance company that he needed to buy a new crane for the scrapyard, and came away with an HP agreement for the required amount.

There were two major FF1600 championships in Britain, the RAC and Esso, which ran in parallel. Most well-financed drivers did both, which meant tackling over 30 races in a season. Since Taylor's team was based at Silverstone, Eddie was restricted to the slightly less prestigious Esso events, which nearly all took place at the Northants track. He also found somewhere to live locally.

'Many years later he told me that he didn't have enough money to heat the place,' says Clifton Hughes. 'At one stage it was so cold he didn't get out of bed for three days! It was pretty tough for him at the beginning.'

At the tracks, Eddie came across some familiar faces including Hill, Herbert and Gachot. There was also a promising young Brit called Mark Blundell who'd won everything in junior FF1600 in 1984. Murray Taylor's F3 programme was headed by Andrew Gilbert-Scott, the winner of the 1983 Festival which Eddie had watched from the sidelines.

'I'd never actually heard of Eddie before,' recalls Gilbert-Scott. 'He just looked like a spotty young kid when he came over. But he was quick straight away, naturally quick.'

The Mondiale was not a great car, but there was some early promise. In the first race on 3 March Eddie finished fourth, behind Blundell, veteran John Village and Hill, and a month later he took pole and led, only to lose out to Hill and Herbert on the way to an eventual third. There were a few more respectable results, but in June it all came grinding to a halt. Team owner Taylor made it plain that he thought Eddie was not going to make it, and the deal went sour. The Irvines now had no car, no money and, as Ed noted, '. . . I still had to pay for my crane!'

'Murray Taylor ended up going back to New Zealand,' says Gilbert-Scott. 'I don't know why and I don't know what happened, but that was that.'

For a few weeks Eddie was on the sidelines, until he organised a drive elsewhere — as team-mate to Herbert. Mike Thompson, boss of the fledgling Quest marque, was keen to get another good driver aboard to help spread the message. The Irvine/Herbert combination would be a strong one today, never mind in a FF1600 team. Eddie never really got to grips with the Quest, which had an unusual suspension design. But then few drivers who tried it did — apart from Herbert. It was a strange twist on the Schumacher set-up conundrum which both drivers would face in years ahead.

'Our car always favoured the smooth driver,' recalls Thompson, who doubled as Herbert's manager. 'It wasn't good for Eddie's style — he was always a hang-it-out merchant in those days. I think it was because of the Mondiale, which was always oversteering. If that's what happens with the first real car you drive, you tend to think that's the way they're all supposed to handle. Johnny was very smooth, but Eddie was quite good at feedback. The thing about Johnny was that he never gave us any feedback. With Eddie, for all his cavalier attitude, he could think a lot, even in those days. If he said there was something wrong, he was normally right. Out of the car he was as good as gold, but he was younger then and perhaps hadn't worked out what he could get away with! He was a good laugh, and he always gave his all. He was very irreverent, which I liked.

'The problem for Eddie was that Johnny got the best of everything, but he had a lot of faith in his own ability and it wouldn't have bothered him. The only doubt I always had was that I felt that any time he could have said, "bugger it, this is too much like hard work," and gone off and done something else. I don't think he would have sacrificed everything to become an F1 driver.'

It was during the Quest period that, as a junior reporter for *Autosport*, I first came across Eddie at Thruxton. That day I also met Herbert, Blundell and Hill. Damon was in a sorry state having written off his loaned Ford Escort on the way to the track!

After five inconclusive outings with Quest, Eddie went his own way again in mid-September: 'I couldn't get on with it. The car kept breaking on me — at Cadwell Park the suspension broke three times in three days. It was nice of them to give me a chance, but it didn't do either of us any good'. He was on the sidelines until the Festival, when he turned up in his old Mondiale, loaned for the weekend by its new owner, Ulster real estate agent Hector Lester. The weekend started well when he qualified on pole for his heat, and finished second to RAC champion Gachot. In his quarter final he spun down to seventh after hitting oil, and in the semi was eliminated when he hit a spinning car. After the previous year's performance, it was a great disappointment. Herbert, meanwhile, took the big prize.

Eddie was voted the most promising newcomer by the 500MRCI, the Kirkistown race organiser. His FF1600 rivals had far more experience. (Ian Lynas)

Mondiale still wanted to give Eddie a hand, and offered him a car for the BBC Grandstand FF2000 winter series at Brands. The first outing was the week after the Festival, and it was his first chance to get to grips with wings and slick tyres. It didn't last long; early in practice Eddie had nowhere to go when another car spun at Paddock and they collided head on. He cut a forlorn figure afterwards as he surveyed the wreckage. 'My first ever three laps in a two-litre,' he told me. 'It can only get better from here!'

Eddie had to drive straight back to Bangor to get the chassis repaired, and after missing the next round was back in mid-November for the last two races. In the first he qualified an impressive ninth of 25 starters, and in the race he battled with Herbert, who'd also stepped up a category. In the final round he rose to sixth until dropping back after a collision.

By now Eddie had struck up a friendship with Martin Spence, boss of Auriga Racing Engines, a popular source of FF1600 powerplants. Spence had large premises in Dartford known as Brise's Yard, the place having once been owned by the family of Tony Brise, who was killed in Graham Hill's plane crash in 1975. Eddie started to make a living selling cars his Dad sent over from Ireland, usually bread-and-butter stuff like Ford Fiestas and Escorts, and for the next few years Spence's garage became a base for this

31

fund-raising venture. He also found somewhere to live nearby; Kent would be his home for a while.

'I can remember the place he was staying in,' says Stephen Patton. 'You had to see it to believe it. The guy had all these cats about the place, and it was stinking, so it was! But it was cheap, and Eddie was happy enough.'

For 1986, Eddie acquired an old truck and a used Van Diemen RF85 — although it turned out to be rather more used than he suspected — and with engines from Spence he set up his own team. Cousin Phillip was his mechanic, despite a serious lack of experience, while Tom Hicks, a friend of Eddie's parents, helped organise the effort. Hicks had contacts with a local newspaper, the *Gravesend and Dartford Extra*, and managed to get his driver regular coverage. To the loyal readers he

Whoops! Eddie goes flying during qualifying for his first race in England, 28 October 1984. (Andrew Charman)

soon became 'Our Eddie,' with little mention of his Irish origin.

'He's not really much different now to what he was then,' says Spence. 'He was obviously spirited, and not hard to get on with by any stretch of the imagination. If he wasn't going well, he wouldn't blame everything round him. He'd look at himself and see how he could improve. You either liked him or got pissed off by him. I don't know what I must have done for him, but one particular day he said to me, "if I ever get to F1 I'll buy you a Ferrari!" I'm still waiting . . .'

Spence emphasises one aspect of Eddie which has served him well: he's always formed a bond with the guys who work on his car. 'He appreciated me spending time on the engines. On the other end of the scale I've seen prima donnas who are an immediate turn-off; little nobodies thinking they're going to become something. Any mechanic or engine builder feels more obliged to work with someone if they're down-to-earth.'

Eddie made a spectacular debut at Brands Hatch: 'We put the engine in

the night before the race in the street in Swanley. Half of the garage was owned by Auriga, and half by a racing team. And the team wouldn't let me take my car through their half of the garage so I could put the engine in! I set fastest lap, got up to third, and it went to my head and I spun off'.

It soon became clear that the RF85 was not the best investment Eddie had made, and it was no match for the up-to-date cars used by drivers with proper funding and professional support. Also, the 'team' was hardly well drilled. At Snetterton the Van Diemen fell out of the truck when both Eddie and cousin Phillip thought the other was holding it, and the pair sheepishly looked around to see if anyone else had noticed. Once Eddie came in from practice to find the remains of a plastic watering can wrapped around a driveshaft — Phillip had left it there after topping up the radiator! Despite all this, he caught the eye with a third at Cadwell Park, a fourth at Thruxton and a good run in the prestigious race supporting the British GP at Brands Hatch, exactly 10 years after the Hunt/Lauda battle.

He did things in that old heap of crap that made you realise the guy was quick

---

Eddie had an ally at Van Diemen's Snetterton factory in the form of John Uprichard, who'd joined as sales manager at the end of 1985. A savvy Ulsterman, Uprichard had raced in Irish FF1600 and was a friend of the Irvine family.

'I knew his father Edmund because he was in the motor trade, always wheeling and dealing, which is what we'd always done. Loads of us used to sell cars to pay for our motor racing. In those days you could do it yourself if you made enough money to pay for your tyres and your entry fees, and a few bits and pieces. When I came to England I had a house four or five miles away from the Van Diemen factory, and Eddie used to come round and stay there, sleep on the floor, things like that.

'His car was a rough old thing. It was always breaking, always bits falling off, things going wrong with it. It would break down, never finish races. He was always coming round here begging and borrowing bits, and everybody got to know him. He was a bit of a character. The other thing was he'd go quickly in that car, albeit he never got any results. He did things in that old heap of crap that made you realise the guy was quick. I don't think anybody knew how quick he really was. He'd show flashes of great speed.'

At Van Diemen Eddie soon got to know Malcolm 'Puddy' Pullen, ace Formula Ford mechanic. In 1981 Puddy had looked after Ayrton Senna,

Right *Looking very pleased with himself — Eddie at age 20.* (Autosport)

and tended various young hopefuls who drove the coveted works Van Diemens. He took an immediate liking to Eddie, and was happy to help out after hours.

'The thing was just a wreck. I remember thinking how the hell can that boy drive the thing? It had bent (suspension) rockers on it, the brake pads were down to the metal, that sort of thing. I stuck the rockers in the press and straightened them out, as he didn't have any money for new ones.'

Eddie was grateful for all the help he could get: 'Puddy was giving me little bits, second-hand nosecones and wishbones and things like that. As the year went on things would get knocked and they'd fall off. Probably by the end of the year the car was miles underweight because there was no bodywork left on it'.

At Oulton Park in September Eddie and his dad first got to know Roland Ratzenberger, a tall amiable Austrian with whom he often seemed to do battle. Having been a mechanic, Roland knew his way around the Van Diemen chassis, and generously volunteered to help set up his rival's car in the paddock. It certainly ran better, but in the race Eddie had the biggest accident of his career to date, hitting the bank at the daunting Knickerbrook corner.

First time out with slicks and wings. Eddie tries Mondiale's FF2000 car in the 1985 Grandstand series. (Autosport)

Eddie dives inside Roland Ratzenberger with his faithful Van Diemen in 1986. Already the tail is half missing . . . (Autosport)

'I know it's not all straight,' he noted on returning to the pits. In fact the car was totally destroyed; he was back to square one, with just a pile of bits to his name. As in the previous year, the British FF1600 championship season ended with Eddie on the sidelines. But again, Irish supporter Hector Lester came to the rescue. He'd replaced his ex-Irvine Mondiale with a new Van Diemen RF86 and allowed Eddie to race this at the Festival. The weekend started badly when he managed only seventh in the heat. That put him in the middle of the grid for the quarter final. He fought up to seventh, and then had to repeat the charge from midfield in the semi, and again in the final, in which he managed eighth. The future still looked bleak, but the Festival led to an offer to do the BBC Grandstand FF2000 series for Talon, a small marque which, like Mondiale and Quest, had failed to break the Reynard/Van Diemen stranglehold. Talon boss Richard Martin, notable in the paddock for his shaggy hair and beard, had given Herbert a run the previous year. Showing a good eye for talent, he then chose Eddie.

'One can call the Talon a fiasco, I suppose,' admits Martin. 'As a swan-song we wanted to prove to ourselves that we hadn't built a total dog of a car. Martin Spence came up with an engine, and at the time Eddie was sitting around his workshop, dealing in second-hand cars from Ireland. Somehow it was decided that he would drive the thing. I think at the time he didn't have much in the way of prospects, but I thought he was good or I

The works Talon gave Eddie a chance to shine in the 1986 Grandstand series (Autosport)

wouldn't have bothered putting him in the car. With him it was a laugh and a joke; he was a jack the lad, really.'

It was a drive, but not quite what Eddie wanted.

'All I had was a toolbox with half a dozen spanners in it,' says Martin, 'and I was running it on my own, holding the car together with tape and rivets. We got old tyres off other people when they declared them junk. It really was a cobbled together piece.'

In the first outing Eddie hauled the car up to a respectable ninth, and then second time out, on a damp track, he qualified a stunning fifth in a strong field of 25. In the race he crashed, but made amends by finishing sixth in the next round, where he qualified just behind teenage Canadian hotshoe Paul Tracy. It was a remarkable effort on a zero budget.

'By then I had to literally borrow £10 from my father to put fuel in my car to get to the circuit,' says Martin. 'The nice thing was Eddie's old man. We were having the usual drink in the bar afterwards and he walked up to me and slipped a £50 note in my pocket, nothing more said.' In an interview a year later, Eddie thanked Martin as 'the first person who really listened to me. The Talon itself was a very good car, very forgiving. But money was a real problem. What everybody else was throwing away, we would use!'

The series over, Eddie still had no prospects, other than a return to the family business. But there was one hope: with many other FF1600 talents moving up to F3, the prime Duckhams Van Diemen seat was still open. Eddie had to convince boss Ralph Firman that he was the man.

'Puddy had brought Eddie to my attention,' says Firman. 'He'd been running around in an old heap of rubbish that was half-prepared, and Puddy tried to give him a hand to set it up. We knew the lack of expertise in the preparation, shall we say, and for him to be going that well, he had to be good.'

Uprichard recalls: 'At the end of 1986 Eddie had given up on it. I'm sure he made the decision that his motor racing was over. But I think he did enough in the Festival and in that Grandstand series to catch Ralph's eye. Paul Warwick had won the junior championships and was in line for the Duckhams car, but he decided to miss out senior FF1600 and go straight to FF2000. Then there were various reasons why the others didn't come together. Steve Robertson wanted to do his own thing, and Tomas Mezera had no money. I think Eddie probably told a porky pie and said he had some!'

As usual, money was a stumbling block. The much coveted drive was heavily subsidised, and again Eddie had to come up with around £10,000, which was about 10,000 more than he had: 'At that stage I couldn't afford it, but the car business was starting to take off so I thought I should be able to scrape the money together'.

He was still in the frame in January 1987.

'I remember sitting on the stand at the Racing Car Show at Alexandra Palace,' says Uprichard. 'Ralph had come for the trade day and the Friday, but he didn't like the weekend because the public was there. Eddie had been there on the trade day, and then came back on the weekend to see Ralph, and of course he'd gone home. Eddie said, "Ralph told me to speak to him at the weekend about the drive." I said, "hold on," so we phoned Ralph from the stand, and I said "Eddie Irvine's here about the drive". Ralph said, "make his day — tell him he's got it."'

CHAPTER THREE

Van Diemen's land

IF THERE WAS a single event which sent Eddie Irvine on his unstoppable progress to the top of motorsport, this was it. Securing the works Van Diemen drive was the first of a series of solid gold opportunities that would land in his lap in the coming years. Eddie was only 21, but including his early steps in Ireland, 1987 would be his fifth season in FF1600, well above average, and with Van Diemen behind him, he was under pressure to get the job done.

Richard Peacock, who'd followed Eddie's career since he first came to the Kirkistown school, says that he actually benefited by staying in the category: 'One of the things that probably helped him most is that he had the brains to stick in FF1600 for as long as possible, rather than this foolish habit people have now of doing a season of this, a season of that, and you've got all these retired racing drivers at 19 years old.

'Eddie was very, very clever. Although he struggled often on very restricted budgets, sleeping in the back of vans in the paddock at Brands, he actually got himself plenty of driving and plenty of practice. In any other sport that you wanted to take seriously, you would practice every day, or three times a week. He got so much out of Formula Ford, whereas so many people's careers have been destroyed by trying to move up categories when they perhaps didn't have the budget or the experience'.

Eddie certainly got mileage with Van Diemen. For a works driver, testing opportunities were virtually limitless, and all told he would compete in some 35 races in 1987. That said, the season did not get off to a great start.

Right *Christmas comes early! Eddie couldn't believe his luck when he landed the Duckhams Van Diemen drive.* (Autosport)

He won the first race at Thruxton on the road, but in a crackdown on speeding under yellow flags the top four drivers were all disqualified, fined £120 and had their licences endorsed. At the start of the second event at Mallory Park, pole man Eddie was eased into the barrier by Antonio Simoes, who went on to win the race. Eddie was furious, and his case was supported by no less a person than Derek Bell, the multiple Le Mans winner. Here spectating, he had happened to film the start of the FF1600 race with his new video camera.

'Ralph wasn't there,' remembers Uprichard, 'and Eddie wanted to protest Simoes. We were up with the stewards. Simoes was thrown out, and some-body in a non-Van Diemen won it. When we got back, Ralph said, "when you're there and I'm not, never ever let Puddy or any of our drivers protest a Van Diemen customer — Puddy may have his loyalties to Eddie, but at the end of the day your loyalties are to Van Diemen, and Simoes and his team are Van Diemen!"'

Next time out at Thruxton, Eddie's race ended in an accident . . . with Simoes. Then his season started to come together. Over the Easter weekend he won three times in three starts at Oulton Park and Silverstone, and he never looked back. Every week brought more victories, poles and fastest laps. Between races Eddie would hang around the Van Diemen factory, and sometimes he got a little encouragement from meeting previous works driver Ayrton Senna, who dropped in to see his old team while on his way to or from nearby Lotus.

Only the occasional mechanical problem kept Eddie off the top spot. Chief rivals Simoes and Alain Menu were usually left trailing in his wake. Swiss Menu, who would later find fame in the British Touring Car Championship, was the works Reynard driver. He was the man Eddie really had to beat, and they had some wild battles. However, a weekend in August provided a shocking reminder of the dangers of the sport, even at this humble level. It started on the Saturday, when Eddie had a big accident at Oulton Park.

'The two of us went off into the distance,' Menu recalls. 'I was actually quicker, but he was blocking me. After a while I thought "OK, I'm going to try now". I went round the outside of the Shell Hairpin. He went more and more to the left, I was going to run out of road, so I stayed there and we touched. He rolled and I spun, and that was that. We had some memorable fights that year.'

Following some frantic overnight repair work by Puddy, Eddie was ahead again at Donington on the Sunday, leaving Menu and Quest driver Peter Rogers dicing for second place. They collided, and Rogers was killed after a violent impact with the barriers. Pete had been in Eddie's first Festival heat back in 1984 and, like Eddie, he had a supportive, racing-mad family and had always struggled to find a drive. That day they had been neighbours in the paddock and spent some time chatting.

Peter Rogers' death was a profound shock, but for Eddie the show went on and the wins kept coming. He secured the main RAC title with ease. In the Esso version Menu was still in with a shout at the Silverstone finale. However, the Reynard man's hopes ended when he was T-boned at the first corner by Jose Cordova, Eddie's team-mate. Now a double champion, Eddie certainly made his mark on the Van Diemen personnel.

'He enjoyed his life,' recalls Puddy. 'He was one of the lads — definitely not the first one to go to bed at night! He liked to go out, go to discos, go drinking or whatever, but when it came to race day, he was always professional. People ask me, "who was the best driver you've ever run — Senna?" I say Eddie Irvine. I rated him very, very highly. The first lap on cold tyres he was very quick. By the time everyone was sorted out, he was gone. The first lap used to win him everything.'

Uprichard agrees. 'When it came to the motor racing there was no messing about. The one thing he could always do was put that first lap in. As soon as the lights went on he could do a time on the first lap, and always come round in the lead. And he was always a good qualifier.'

But how did young Irvine rate overall?

'We've had lots and lots of really good drivers,' says Firman. 'I think Eddie falls into that outstanding group, a cut above the rest, like your Ayrtons. I worked with Emerson Fittipaldi in my early days as a mechanic,

Familiar sight: Eddie leads the field away at Brands. Ringo Hine (14) and Alain Menu (hidden) give chase. (Autosport)

and he was outstanding. I always felt Eddie came into that bracket. He gives that impression of being totally laid back — whether he is or not, one will never know. He enjoys his life, and he always has. He was a bit of a nutty Irishman really, full of fun. I enjoyed the year he was here.'

With the titles secure, the Festival was next on the agenda, but before it Eddie had an even more important date in his diary.

At that time Marlboro was pumping big money into the junior categories, and from 19 to 22 October the company held a four day test at Donington to determine who would get the budgets for 1988. Up for grabs were two seats in F3000 with Onyx and ORECA, a drive in the British F3 series with West Surrey Racing (JJ Lehto was already secure at Pacific Racing), and two places with a new team in the recently announced GM/Lotus Euroseries. Eddie was a last-minute nomination by journalists who advised the British arm of Marlboro owners Philip Morris, and was surprised to be put straight onto the F3 list rather than that for Opel/Lotus, which might have been more logical:

'I thought I was going there for a FF2000 test, which was fair enough, but they wanted me to do an F3 test. I thought, shit, there's no chance I'm going to get this. It's not fair. I tried to talk them into letting me do the FF2000 test, but they wouldn't let me. The others had all done F3'.

The talent on offer that week was remarkable. British F3 champion Johnny Herbert pulled out due to 'prior commitments' — a Camel-backed F3000 drive with Eddie Jordan — so left vying for the F3000 seats were Jean Alesi, Martin Donnelly, Bertrand Gachot, Bernd Schneider, Andrea Chiesa, Volker Weidler and Enrico Bertaggia, all of whom would eventually make it to F1, with varying degrees of success.

Joining Eddie aboard the ex-Gachot F3 car were Mark Blundell, Gianni Morbidelli, Peter Kox and Jason Elliott. The GM hopefuls, who tested an FF2000 car, were Mika Hakkinen, Allan McNish, Michael Bartels, Jean-Marc Gounon, Ralf Kelleners and Frank Kramer. The list of judges was also distinguished. Marlboro had hired James Hunt to supervise its young drivers, and the 1976 World Champion was joined on the panel by McLaren supremo Ron Dennis, along with F3000 team bosses Mike Earle (from Onyx) and Hughes de Chaunac (of ORECA). Dick Bennetts of West Surrey was also on hand to advise.

John Uprichard takes up the story: 'Eddie told me later that all the drivers were in the hotel in their shirts and ties, sitting there with their fathers and all being sensible, trying to cultivate the image with Marlboro and all the rest of it. It came to 9pm and they were all saying, "we must go to bed now and have an early night". I guess Eddie went out instead, and he snuck back into the bar again at midnight or something, and Hunt was there. James said, "what are you doing down here, shouldn't you be having

He's done it! Eddie sprays the champagne after the magnificent 1987 Festival win. (Colin Taylor)

an early night because you're testing tomorrow?". And Eddie said to James, "well, I've been nightclubbing." Hunt said, "you're my man!" I think the two gelled quite well. They forged a relationship then which did him no harm . . .'

When the test sessions got under way Blundell soon ruled himself out when the car dug in and rolled after what would have otherwise been a harmless spin.

Eddie had to use WSR's spare car. After making some set-up changes he was quicker than the others, albeit by just 0.05s, and he did everything right.

'It's difficult with those things to work out how to choose a driver,' says Bennetts. 'Sometimes a guy may be tenth on a test like that, but there will be ability in there. I know Mike Earle was in favour of him, but I think Ron was a bit reserved, because Eddie wouldn't be Ron's type of character, not clean cut and quiet! The one thing that impressed us was he wasn't affected by anything. That was quite important — self confidence.'

Ron Dennis says he has no memory of the day, but Mike Earle agrees that Eddie impressed from the start.

'He exuded the confidence that's stayed with him all the way through. He had that healthy belief in his own ability, and didn't have to worry too much about what other people thought. He was quick in the car and had it all together, but what impressed me was that when it came to the interview bit, he just told you what he thought. He came over as someone who loved what he was doing. That was great.

'After he'd done his 10–15 minute interview, James said he had an attitude that was not unlike him at that age. It was the same sort of irreverence for the established members of the motor racing firmament. Eddie felt he was as good as anybody that was around at that time, and couldn't see any reason why he should worry about it. Everyone else was trying to give this considered approach to the socio-economic state of the world, he just stood up and said, "I'm a racing driver, I know I'm good, and I know I'm going to get there," or words to that effect! Even Ron liked him — he said he was refreshing.'

Intriguingly, that very week *Autosport* carried its first profile on Eddie. Writer Patrick Young noted: 'In the longer term, Irvine would be content to secure any reasonably remunerative post in top-line racing. Sensibly, he retains a degree of pessimism regarding an eventual seat in F1 . . .'

Marlboro would not announce its decision for a few weeks. In the meantime Eddie had the Festival to think about. As works Van Diemen driver

Party time after the Festival. Mechanic 'Puddy' joins Eddie at the start of a long night, while the winner's proud grandfather Harry Irvine looks on. (Autosport)

Leading again, this time in the 1987 Grandstand series. Steve Robertson heads the chasing pack. (Autosport)

and double national champion, he was firm favourite. As he told me before the event, 'I can only lose the Festival — everyone else can win it!'

He needn't have worried. He took pole for his heat on Saturday, and won it easily. On Sunday he won the quarter final, the semi (where he came across Finnish newcomer Mika Salo for the first time), and then dominated the final to win from Menu and Coyne. It was the first win for a works Van Diemen, and an Irishman, since Tommy Byrne took Senna's car to victory in 1981. That was cause for a double celebration. In the stands that day was Harry Irvine, Eddie's grandfather. Well into his eighties, he'd rarely had the chance to see the boy in action.

'What can you say about an Irishman at the Festival?' says Uprichard. 'If you can remember it, it would be a bad sign! Everyone got pissed afterwards. It was tremendous as far as the Irish contingent was concerned.'

'I got wrecked,' says Puddy. 'I think we all did! That was just brilliant. He was a popular winner. He was the people's choice. Everybody liked Eddie Irvine.'

Eddie's season was not over yet. He was given the works Van Diemen, also Duckhams-sponsored, for the BBC Grandstand FF2000 series. He missed the first round, held on the Festival weekend, but took pole and won in the second and third races. The season ended on a low note. After finishing second in the penultimate Grandstand FF2000 race, he went into the double points finale just four points behind series leader Jonathan Bancroft. Tension was high, and the race was stopped after Bancroft hit the barrier on the way to Paddock Bend; Eddie won the re-start, but was later judged to have forced his rival off. He was disqualified from the win, lost the title, had his licence endorsed for 'reckless driving' and was fined £100. Still, his win total for the year was 21, plus the two other races from which he was disqualified. Putting that into context, the next eight seasons up to his arrival at Ferrari in 1996 produced just five race victories.

The £100 would have come in useful, for Eddie still had to pay for the Duckhams drive, as Uprichard recalls.

'At the end of the season when he came to settle up, he said, "I'm sorry I can't pay you, what about a management contract — I'll give you 10% of everything I earn in the future." Ralph said, "no, I could have done that with Senna, Gugelmin, Moreno and everyone else that's been through here. Our business is selling racing cars. You know perfectly well that we'll end up in court and you'll say you did that under duress. We'll only fall out over it." But Eddie always said, "when I make it, I'll pay you."'

Firman himself reckons Eddie was offering a more generous 20%!

'He was supposed to pay, to the best of my knowledge, 10 grand,' recalls Ralph. 'And he'd given me about three. I pushed him and pushed him and pushed him. It wasn't so much for the money as much as the principle of the thing. These guys have to realise they've got to pay for things. He said, "I can't, I can't, I can't," and that he would pay when he had the money.'

It would be a long wait. Had Eddie won the Cellnet Award, a prestigious prize for young British drivers, he would have been in a better economic position. But the star-studded panel wasn't impressed, as Eddie recalled many years later: 'It was rather disappointing, financially more than anything else. They asked me what have you done? They obviously hadn't got a clue. Maybe they were judging my interview style, but what the hell has that got to do with whether you're going to make it in motor racing'.

In any case, Eddie's thoughts already lay with the year ahead. A couple of weeks after the Festival triumph, and during his Grandstand FF2000 campaign at Brands, Marlboro announced its plans for 1988. The F3000 drives went to Alesi and Weidler, the GM/Lotus seats to McNish and Hakkinen, and the F3 deal was Eddie's.

In stepping from Van Diemen to West Surrey Racing, Eddie was following the path trodden by Senna just five years earlier. The Brazilian was not the only big name to have driven for Dick Bennetts; others included Jonathan Palmer, Stefan Johansson, Mauricio Gugelmin and Bertrand Gachot.

Eddie would be up against some strong opposition in F3. Most of the top drivers had experience in the category, including Cellnet team-mates Damon Hill and Martin Donnelly, and Bowman's Gary Brabham. Also in the field were old sparring partners such as Ratzenberger, Bancroft and Menu, and Paul Warwick, brother of F1 star Derek. But the man Eddie really wanted to beat was fellow newcomer JJ Lehto, who had graduated from FF2000 together with his Pacific team. At the time Lehto was the golden boy, and it already seemed certain that Marlboro would ease the Finn's passage all the way to F1.

Eddie was also keen to outpace his WSR team-mate, former FF1600 rival Simoes. The highly-rated Portuguese driver was expected to give Eddie a hard time, but his challenge soon faded. He rolled a car in testing even before the season started, and was the first of a string of unfortunate Irvine team-mates who would find themselves eased out of the limelight.

'Simoes was quick and wild,' says Dick Bennetts. 'Eddie just took the piss out of him, and made him worse. He's good at winding up other people. I don't think he always means to, but that's his nature.'

He was still buying and selling cars, and that's how he was living

Just as important as driver ability was the 'package.' Ralt and Reynard were evenly matched in the chassis wars, but a fierce battle was fought among the engine makers, with VW (Spiess), Toyota (TOM'S) and Alfa (Novomotor) the contestants. Eddie's Ralt RT32, as engineered by Bennetts, was a match for anyone. But his Alfa engines were a weak link. Dick explains:

'We had the works Alfas, and some of them were good and some not so good. That was one of the weaknesses that year. You'd put one in and it would be OK, put another in and it would be a dog, so it was a bit frustrating'.

To further complicate matters, Lehto's Reynard had a demon Toyota which gave him an extra edge on the competition. 'We could be equal quickest in testing when they had their normal engine in,' recalls Bennetts. 'Then they'd put in their race engine, and always find that extra tenth and beat us.'

From the start of the season, Lehto was the dominant force. He won the first race at Thruxton, ahead of Donnelly and Hill. Eddie, meanwhile, made a good F3 debut with fourth place. Next time out at Silverstone Lehto won again, but Eddie qualified second, made the better start and led the first lap before the Finn shot past. Two races later at Brands Eddie qualified second to Donnelly, but the two Ulstermen clashed at Druids while disputing the lead, and Irvine trailed home 16th. Next time out at Donington Eddie took pole and led until overheating forced him to slow, allowing Donnelly and

Kid with a new toy. Eddie looks happy after sampling Marlboro's F3 car at the Donington test. (Autosport)

Sibling rivalry? Lehto forces his way inside Eddie at Silverstone. The two battled for much of 1988. (Autosport)

Lehto past. It seemed only a matter of time before Eddie won a race, but somehow luck didn't go his way.

'We had a couple of mechanical failures,' says Bennetts. 'He was leading at Donington, and I remember Gary Brabham had been off on the grass, and of course Eddie picked up all the grass and it cooked the engine. On a lot of occasions we were right up there but it didn't show in the results because we had problems.'

Eddie impressed in the car, but still had a lot to learn out of it. 'You couldn't sit down and have a good technical discussion with him. That's often the problem when drivers jump from FF1600 to F3; a different driving technique is required. He'd just drive the car to the limit, and in those days couldn't say, "it's too soft at the front or too soft at the rear or it's rolling". He just knew if it understeered or oversteered. You can't expect too much more from some guys at an early stage of their careers.

> *Everyone was there, ready to race, and Eddie hadn't arrived — he was hard work at times!*

'He was a bit hard to control at times. He was still buying and selling road cars, and that's how he was living, because he had no extra income. One Sunday he looked at the map and thought "I'll nip in and buy this road car and go on to Silverstone". So he detoured off somewhere, and Sod's law, the car broke down. He arrived with minutes to spare when he should have been there two hours before the race!

'The other classic was when the clocks changed, and he forgot to change his. Again he almost missed the race. We'd told him, "don't forget Ed, the clocks change tonight". "Yeah, yeah, yeah." Everyone was there ready to go racing, and he hadn't turned up. He was hard work at times.'

While the race engines were a disappointment, a positive side effect was that Eddie got his hands on a brand new Alfa road car, a major step up from the usual second-hand stock he travelled around in. On one occasion, while driving to Snetterton, he was forced to make an unscheduled stop at the Van Diemen factory.

'I remember he came swooping into this place,' recalls John Uprichard, 'and drove straight round the back to the race shop and closed the door. The cops were chasing him for speeding on the A11! He sat there talking to everybody until it all calmed down.'

Auriga engines boss Martin Spence also had experience of Eddie's Alfa antics.

'One night I was playing squash. It was about 10.30pm. There was a bang on the back of the squash court, and it was him. He had the courtesy Alfa, and he had to take it back to Dover, I think it was. He wanted me to follow him and bring him back. I said to him, "have you checked this out with my missus?" He said, "yeah it's OK, no problem." I followed him all the way down to Dover like a mad man, trying to keep behind him, and when I got home that night found out he hadn't even spoken to my wife. She was going crackers wondering where the hell I'd gone!'

Bennetts had also arranged an Alfa estate car for himself. One day he made the mistake of loaning it to his young driver for a trip to famed engine builder Novomotor.

'Around June time we had an engine due for a rebuild and I said, "why don't you take it down to Italy, meet the man, see the engine being rebuilt, watch it on the dyno, and he might do a bit of extra work on it for us?" He agreed to do it, so I loaned him my Alfa Sportwagon, which was virtually brand new. He said, "can I take a mate?", and I said, "no problem, he can keep you company". He'd never been to Italy, and I thought he'd arrive there in the Sportwagon with the Alfa engine strapped in the back, and it would be a great PR exercise.

'This didn't come out until later, but apparently they'd been to a night-club in the Cambridge area. They took off in the middle of the night, and all I found out was that at 5am, somewhere in France, a black BMW pulled

Eddie tries to find a way past Damon Hill at Brands. No, it didn't work . . .
(Autosport)

out of a side road — it had to be black — and they swerved to avoid it and clouted the side of a house!

'I got a call, "we've had a little bit of a shunt, Dickie". Great! It had all the side ripped out of it, but they managed to get it going with a bit of help from someone. They'd got big bars and hammers and straightened out the mudguards and suspension. Anyway, they eventually got to Novomotor. I spoke to them the next day and it was, "the food's shit, they don't speak English, but the beer's all right!" That was the attitude in those days. It's kind of funny when you see him end up at Ferrari.'

Lehto meanwhile ran away with the championship, holding off a late challenge from Gary Brabham. Despite being part of the Marlboro 'family', JJ and Eddie were not big buddies.

'He was very arrogant, no style, no sort of respect for anybody,' says Lehto. 'I was always together with Damon, Paul Warwick and those guys. Eddie was from another planet. Nobody could really discuss anything with him. That year I would say Donnelly was very good and strong, and Gary Brabham was very good. They were definitely the best. Eddie for sure had the best equipment.'

JJ's views may be a little harsh, for everyone else acknowledges that the Alfas were a handicap. Eddie didn't win a race, but ended the F3 season with five second places to his name. He made very few mistakes, finished in the top six in 13 of his 18 starts, and secured fifth place in the championship behind Lehto, Brabham, Hill and Donnelly. Eddie knew he could have done better: 'The problem was the Alfa engine. We were trying to make up for a deficit, which you can't do in motor racing. You've got to have it all right, or you're not going to make it. Dick had the car very well sorted out, but we still couldn't win races. We just didn't have the grunt'.

With the points race over, there still remained a couple of extra, high profile events. Eddie shone in both. The Cellnet Superprix was a much-hyped non-championship event at Brands, featuring a compulsory pit stop for tyres. Eddie was leading the wet event when a misfire struck. In the pits, a rare miscommunication within the WSR team saw his car fitted with a mixture of wets and slicks. Once that was sorted out, Eddie was again fastest on the drying track, although well out of contention.

Next on the agenda was November's Macau GP, but before that Eddie had to attend another Marlboro test, this time at Imola. While a second year of F3 in 1989 might have made sense, the continuous flow of talent up the Marlboro ladder meant there was pressure to push Eddie straight into F3000. Having shone in the new GM/Lotus series, Hakkinen and McNish were in line for the cigarette maker's F3 budget, so the only way for Irvine was up — or out of the programme. Lehto was already guaranteed one F3000 seat, and Eddie had to prove himself worthy of the

Eddie leads the field away in the Cellnet Superprix. A misfire cost him victory.
(Autosport)

second ride. Eddie outlined his thinking the week before the test:

'Some people are advising me to stay in F3 and, hopefully, win next year's championship, but I think it may be better to follow JJ into F3000 for what will be a very competitive season. I don't know Imola and I haven't yet driven an F3000 car, but I'm certainly looking forward to the opportunity'.

The test took place on 8 November, two days before his 23rd birthday. Established Marlboro/Onyx driver Volker Weidler set a base time in his March 88B, and then Emanuele Naspetti (the new Italian F3 champion), Erik Comas (winner of the French title) and Eddie each had a tilt at it. Fastest of the four, albeit by fractions, was Eddie — despite going last, when the brakes and gearbox were all but worn out. Typically, he was totally unfazed by the experience when asked for his first impressions :

'The only thing I found difficult was braking for the slow corners, and getting the car stopped. The fact that I was last out could have something to do with that. Overall though, the car inspires more confidence than an F3 car because it is softer and transmits more feel of what it is doing'.

'He went well,' recalls Onyx boss Mike Earle. 'I said to the people at Philip Morris that for me, the guy was head and shoulders above the others. Not just in the car but out of it as well. He did get in the car last, and it did have one or two problems. The gearbox was a bit shot; you can imagine, after putting three guys who are new to F3000 in it. But he was just mightily impressive.

'It's always difficult to say how you look at drivers and decide if they're good. For me, it's no different to watching any other great sportsman — they've got all the time in the world. A good racing driver is 20 yards ahead of his car, and a bad one is 20 yards behind, sorting out what's happened. Eddie was always 20 yards ahead. I think he was very well aware that he had impressed at the test, and if he went to Macau and went well, he was going to get the drive.'

Macau was, and still is, a major stepping stone for young drivers, and everyone who goes there wants to emulate Senna's masterly winning performance of 1983. The top contenders from the F3 championships in Britain, Italy, France, Germany and Japan are invited, and at the time Eddie raced there, some also stepped back from F3000 and even F1 to take on the youngsters. Newcomers generally have a tough time getting a feel for the fast daunting curves near the sea front and the tight, twisty section through the hills. Eddie promptly put his car on pole — and people took notice.

'When we got to Macau the Alfa finally seemed OK on the avgas they use there,' says Bennetts, 'and it responded better. Eddie got pole and we couldn't believe it! The only crash I can remember that year was on the final lap of qualifying at Macau, when he misread the lap board, having already got pole. I'd told him to do a quick lap, a slow lap and a quick lap, so he could cool the tyres and have a think. He did a 2m 22.6s to go quickest, but there was no radio in those days so we couldn't tell him. Then he did a slow lap which was a 2m 32.1s. He came around with two minutes to go to start his last lap, we had "P1" and "32.1" on the board. He thought it said "22.1", and that it was somebody else's pole time! He went balls out and crashed, and took the left front corner off. I asked what was that about, and he said "I saw that 22.1, and tried to brake later!" I said, "no, that was 32.1, your previous lap!" But as he said, it was his first shunt of the year.'

As usual Eddie had done the job when it mattered: 'Marlboro said "qualify well and you'll be looking good. We know the race is a bit of a lottery". I stuck it on pole, and thought, I can't qualify much better than that! Comas was nowhere'.

A look at the grid shows the scale of Eddie's achievement. Lined up right behind him were Joachim Winkelhock (the German F3 champion), Jean Alesi (stepping in from F3000) and JJ Lehto. Further back could be found interesting names such as Coloni F1 man Gabriele Tarquini, Damon Hill,

Bertrand Gachot, 1987 Macau winner Martin Donnelly, Gianni Morbidelli, Karl Wendlinger, F1 veterans Stefan Johansson and Jan Lammers, and Comas. Eddie and JJ's rivalry was as evident as ever when the first of the two heats got under way.

'I had a shunt at the first corner when I tried to overtake him,' says JJ. 'I went off and hit the wall very hard. That was nothing to do with him; I got a good start and went inside, but it was so slippery there that I couldn't stop at the end of the straight. It was my mistake.'

The race was stopped and restarted. This time Eddie was under no threat. Bennetts recalls:

'He'd actually opened up about a 4s lead over Jean Alesi, which I was over the moon with, but he came across a backmarker and only ended up winning by about 1.5s. Then in race two, he fluffed the start and panicked. He tried to block out Rickard Rydell, but Eddie finished up banging the wall, not Rydell. I think if he'd bided his time he would have won the race overall.'

Eddie remembers it differently: 'We were 26th fastest on the straight or something, so I knew I had to get into the first corner first or I wouldn't be able to overtake anybody. I was leading, Alesi was on the outside and Rydell on the inside. And he touched my rear wheel and spun me into the armco. End of story'.

With many of the other front-runners, including Alesi, also having problems victory went to the unfancied Enrico Bertaggia, ahead of a reliable Hill. Eddie at least set fastest lap, and consoled himself in the buzzing Macau nightclubs where the drivers could let their hair down. In retrospect, Bennetts says Irvine compared favourably with other star names he's handled in F3.

'Obviously the guys who won the championship were good. Ayrton and Mika Hakkinen I'd still have to say were the two most rawly talented guys. Rubens Barrichello was very good in qualifying, but by then we'd had the Honda engine for three years and everything was in good shape. To be honest, I never dreamt of Eddie making it in F1, because in those days he didn't have the attitude that he wanted to get into F1. All he wanted to do was make money. A bit like Eddie Jordan!'

The Macau performance was more than enough to convince Philip Morris that Irvine deserved to graduate. With Onyx stopping its F3000 programme to enter F1, Marlboro favourites Pacific Racing plugged the gap by stepping straight up from its successful first year in British F3 to running two F3000 Reynards.

This meant that in 1989 Eddie and Lehto would be team-mates . . .

• CHAPTER FOUR •

Bright side of the road

THE 1989 FIA Formula 3000 season kicked off with the International Trophy at Silverstone in April, and among the many friends who'd come to watch Eddie's debut was Clifton Hughes, his Irish FF1600 mentor.

'Here was this car immaculately prepared, all done out in Marlboro colours,' recalls Hughes. 'There were three guys working on the Mugen engine and about four working on the car, dressed up in red and white. We sat on the pit wall watching and I said, "Eddie, this is what we dreamed about when we were at Kirkistown". He looked over at me and said, "I didn't even dream about this"'.

Eddie had arrived in the big time. F3000 was the final step before Grand Prix racing, the training ground for the Formula 1 stars of the future. Like F3, it was at the time well supported by generous sponsors such as Marlboro and Camel, which ensured that most drivers were there purely on merit rather than because they had connections or family money. Many of the leading contenders had already gained F3000 experience, including Alesi, Donnelly, Thomas Danielsson, Mark Blundell, Eric Bernard and Marco Apicella. Apart from Irvine and Lehto, other top newcomers included Comas and Eric van de Poele. All in all, it was an impressive field.

Eddie and JJ had the luxury of having proper funding for their Mugen-engined Reynard 89Ds — but like them the Pacific team was new to the formula and had much to learn. There were 10 races across Europe, and the only circuits known to either drivers or the team were Silverstone, Brands Hatch and Spa, the latter having hosted a British F3 round the year before. Reynard designer Malcolm Oastler was seconded to engineer Eddie's car, while Pacific boss Keith Wiggins looked after Lehto, as he had done previously in FF1600, FF2000 and F3.

Lehto's own strong links to Pacific and 'Wiggy' concerned Eddie. Not unnaturally he considered that the established guy in the team might receive better treatment. On the other hand, he was shrewd enough to know that running alongside Lehto could work in his favour. If he quietly got on with the job and beat the Finn, the applecart would be well and truly upset: 'I wanted to be up against JJ. Everybody thought this guy's Ayrton Senna, and I'd have a good standard to be judged against. Naively I thought if I can beat him I'm in F1. They all thought he was a mega, so then they'd think I was a *mega* mega.'

It was not to be the only time that Eddie made use of being the underdog alongside a feted star.

'No team had ever had two Marlboro cars in F3000 before,' says Wiggins, 'but at that stage we'd been with them for four years and won every championship that we'd done. It was good timing for us. I remember Mike Earle saying, "you bastard, I've been trying to get that for three years!" I think Eddie was quite happy with it at the time. We were a good team; JJ was there, but Eddie's not frightened of being with anybody.'

JJ's manager Keke Rosberg was also able to use his Marlboro contacts to land his protege a testing contract with Ferrari, further boosting his profile. Lehto was seen by many as a future World Champion, and it seemed it was only a matter of time before Rosberg found him a full-time F1 drive. But there were also people within the Philip Morris hierarchy who were keen to see Eddie do well. Not least among them was James Hunt, Marlboro's in-house driver coach and guru. The two iconoclasts had met in F3, when James was an occasional race visitor, but in F3000 their relationship blossomed. Graham Bogle, leading Philip Morris motorsport man and a long-time Irvine supporter, takes up the story:

'James was a very good judge of what it takes to be a racing driver. It gave him a chance to belong, to give something back to the sport, and get enthusiastic about young drivers' careers. It gave him a lot of satisfaction and a lot of motivation. When you see someone learn from coaching and guidance, as Stefano Modena did in F3000, it is very rewarding. There was a good chemistry — drivers relate to drivers. So he was a key player for us in supporting our drivers through good times and bad times. It was very, very successful with a number of drivers, not with all, but Irvine was one of them.

'I think they had a similar ambition and they had a similar sense of fun, and to some extent a simplicity of approach to their work and their surroundings. They were not comfortable with some of the obligations of

Right *Looking glum. The 1989 season started with a run of disastrous races.*
(Autosport)

motorsport, they didn't want to conform. There was that irreverent and appealing characteristic to both of them. And that's why they got on, and that's why they leaned on each other. I think that when Eddie was forming his career he drew upon many of the things that James taught.'

Dubliner David Marren, who worked closely with Hunt and Irvine at Philip Morris, agrees that the relationship was important to Eddie's development.

'Hunt was certainly one of his biggest fans, because Eddie was a very personable bloke and also because James believed that he had all the attributes that were going to make a good driver some day. I found the two personalities very similar.'

Another World Champion, Ayrton Senna, had a — sartorial — influence on Eddie. Until the move up to F3000, Eddie had raced in a plain white helmet, simply not bothering to come up with a personalised colour scheme. For his first F3000 race at Silverstone, he turned up with an uncannily familiar design.

'I thought Senna's helmet was about the most distinctive around at the moment,' he explained. 'Marlboro were keen that I did something more adventurous than plain white. The orange is for Ulster but it was supposed to be the Marlboro dayglo colour. To be honest I prefer the white and I get less buffeting with it!'

Eddie's 1989 season hardly got off to a great start. On his debut at Silverstone, he was 0.3s faster than Lehto in qualifying, but got stranded by an electrical failure on the warm-up lap, and didn't even make the race. At Vallelunga three weeks later he qualified badly after tangling with another car, and had a second collision early in the race. At Pau he was black-flagged, fined US$5000 and excluded for allegedly defending his position too aggressively (against a local driver). 'What was I supposed to do,' he pleaded, 'invite everyone past?'

The only consolation for Eddie was that JJ had hardly set the world alight in the first three races; he had just one fourth to his name, having been disqualified from third at Silverstone due to a rev limiter infringement. All in all, it was a dreadful start for Pacific, as Wiggins explains:

'Looking back on it, because we'd been new to F3 and only done one year and then moved to F3000, to be honest the team didn't really do the best job. But I think we did do a solid job. The Reynard wasn't the best car at that stage, and Jordan had more experience and got the car better sorted than us. We had our moments, but with two drivers who hadn't done F3000 before, new tracks, a new team and a car that needed a bit of work, we just didn't really get it right.'

Things got better at Jerez. Eddie qualified third and ran second behind Bernard until electrical problems intervened. In the fifth round at Enna in

Eddie hustles his Reynard 89D around Dijon. (Zooom)

July he finally saw a chequered flag; only five cars were running at the end of the race, and he finished third. At Brands he had one of the biggest crashes of his career in qualifying, and had another in the race, and was then sixth at Birmingham and ninth at Spa. At that stage Eddie and JJ languished well down the table on five and six points respectively, well below Marlboro's and Pacific's expectations. But Eddie's qualifying performances in particular had impressed his sponsor, and he regularly outpaced Lehto.

'It was a time when JJ was perceived as the rising star,' says Graham Bogle, 'and he really was, to be honest. Eddie was very much a talented driver, but behind Lehto. During the course of that season he really chipped away at his apparent margin of superiority, until he was on a par. If you look at his career to date, he's always done that. He's always chipped away at an apparently superior team-mate, trying to catch up.'

Not that Lehto had anything to worry about. At the end of September, he made an earlier than expected step up to F1 at the Portuguese GP. The new Onyx team fell out with Bertrand Gachot, and JJ was deemed a suitable replacement.

'I had the impression that Eddie was generally quicker,' recalls then Onyx designer Alan Jenkins. 'But we were hearing very good noises about JJ from the people at Ferrari, because he was testing a lot. We needed somebody just to put straight in. I'd known Keke for years, and he was pushing quite hard to allow it to be arranged quickly. JJ fitted the bill and did brilliantly.'

Having arrived at Estoril at very short notice, Lehto just missed the pre-qualifying cut after suffering a suspension breakage. However, not making the race allowed him to jet back to Le Mans to take part in the penultimate F3000 round, where he crashed out on the first lap. Eddie, meanwhile, was an impressive fourth.

A week later, JJ was back in the Onyx at Jerez. This time he made it through pre-qualifying with ease, something which team-mate Stefan Johansson — a lucky third at Estoril — failed to do. In qualifying proper, Lehto impressed by securing 17th place, and running well until the gearbox broke. Sitting watching the grand prix on television at his base in Bromley, Eddie was somewhat bemused by JJ's sudden turn of fortune, having beaten him six–three in F3000 qualifying.

'He wanted to prove a point and show that he was quicker than JJ,' says Wiggins, 'which any sensible driver who believes in himself will do. I think he proved that he was as quick. But there are more things in motor racing that make up the package.'

The next GP was the Japanese, which clashed with the F3000 finale at Dijon. His F1 future secure, JJ headed for Suzuka, leaving up-and-coming Marlboro/WSR F3 star Allan McNish to take over his seat in France. As it turned out, the trip to Japan was wasted, and JJ failed to get through pre-qualifying. Meanwhile, Eddie and James Hunt travelled from Paris to Dijon by train, and had a bit of a party, having met some soldiers along the way. It didn't do Eddie any harm however, for he finished fourth again.

The 1989 season ended with Alesi and Comas equal at the top of the table on 39 points, although Jean got the verdict having won more races. Eddie was down in ninth place on 11 points, while Lehto had just six and was 13th equal.

'To be fair, Eddie did a very good job, there's no doubt about it,' says Wiggins. 'It made me realise that perhaps in F3 he didn't have the right engine, unfortunately. But we weren't in the best position to take advantage as a team, so it was unlucky for him again. I had the feeling that he was seat-of-the-pants and lacked a bit technically. He was just a quick driver, but not always sure why! Give him anything with four wheels and he'd get the best out of it. But having said that we were a bit off — if we'd had a magic driver on feedback it might have helped us with the car.

'He was a very natural guy. Sometimes I didn't think that he would make it, because I didn't think he was perhaps serious enough. He wasn't any good at getting sponsors, and without Marlboro I thought he hadn't got the make-up to make it. Some drivers you get close to, but I don't think I ever

James Hunt was both a friend and mentor to the young Irvine. (Autosport)

Second time at Macau and Eddie rejoins the WSR team. It was a bad weekend. (PR Plus)

got close to Eddie. We'd have a laugh and that was it really. In that first year we had our own problems to get over. I wouldn't say he was a driver I had a heart-to-heart with. He never really expressed much, and I wouldn't know if he was unhappy or not.'

Wiggins says that Eddie never complained about Lehto getting special treatment.

'I think he might have thought that, but he never expressed it, and I certainly didn't feel it. They got on OK. JJ probably felt slightly more pressure, because he'd always been the centre of attention at Pacific. But he was pretty easy going. There was a fair bit of rivalry but I certainly never felt there was anything negative, not like you see in some teams. They just both wanted to be quicker than the other.'

I enjoyed the test, and now know there's no big deal about Formula 1

With the F3000 season over, Eddie stepped back to F3 for another crack at the Macau GP with Marlboro and West Surrey Racing, alongside Allan McNish. Suffering from 'flu, he qualified seventh — immediately behind a pair of promising German rookies called Heinz-Harald Frentzen and Michael Schumacher. His race ended when another car bounced off the tyre wall at the first corner, and Eddie and McNish both piled in. Eddie didn't take the re-start.

'Dick wasn't impressed,' recalls McNish. 'He had two crashed cars and he got a $20,000 fine when they tried to repair mine on the grid! Off the track, I couldn't keep up with Eddie. He was Mr Out-and-about, and I was trying to be professional and go to bed at 9pm.'

There was still one more outing for Eddie in 1989. Marlboro had promised to redress the pro-Lehto balance by arranging an F1 test with Onyx, and in late December he headed south to Paul Ricard for his big opportunity.

'Marlboro were always responsible in the way they worked with young drivers,' says Irvine fan and former Onyx boss Mike Earle. 'They felt that he'd stalled out a bit and needed a little bit more of a push. It was mentioned and we were keen to do it anyway.'

It was only two years since his last FF1600 race, and yet here he was knocking on the door of Grand Prix racing, having just turned 24. Had it gone well, the day could have changed his life, but the run in Johansson's car was anything but career enhancing.

'I'd arranged for him to have the test some two or three months earlier,' says Earle, 'and before it happened, I left the team. So I didn't actually

The works Duckhams drive set Eddie on his way to the top in 1987. (Tom Hicks)

Happy smiling face. Eddie became a fixture on the podium that season. (Tom Hicks)

A crucial day. Eddie impressed WSR boss Dick Bennetts at the October 1987 Marlboro test, and earned an F3 drive. (Autosport)

Eddie led several F3 races in 1988, but never actually won. Here he splashes round Thruxton. (Autosport)

Honeymoon period for the Pacific F3000 team-mates in 1989. Eddie and JJ Lehto didn't always see eye to eye. (Zooom)

Never one to listen to advice, Eddie had mixed fortunes in 1989. (Zooom)

Engineer Malcom Oastler (left) and team boss Keith Wiggins discuss the way round Dijon. The Senna-like helmet design was later toned down. (Zooom)

James Hunt was one of Eddie's strongest supporters in the Marlboro years.
(Zooom)

*New allegiance — Eddie switched cigarette brands to join Eddie Jordan's camp
in 1990.* (Zooom)

Macau 1990: winner Schumacher is flanked by Eddie and Mika Salo. (PR Plus)

Eddie spent a lucrative three years in Japanese F3000. (Author)

Watched by his buddies, Eddie takes the customary pre-race bow at Fuji in 1992.
(Author)

The Cerumo team celebrates victory at Mine in 1992. Boss Sato is third from left and team manager Murayama on the far right.
(Author)

Head of the table! Grub's up in Suzuka for Mika Salo, Mauro Martini (hidden), Jeff Krosnoff, Eddie, and Roland Ratzenberger.
(Author)

Eddie set a stunning pace for Toyota at Le Mans in 1993. (Autosport)

Calm before the storm. Eddie relaxes during qualifying for his F1 debut at Suzuka. (Autosport)

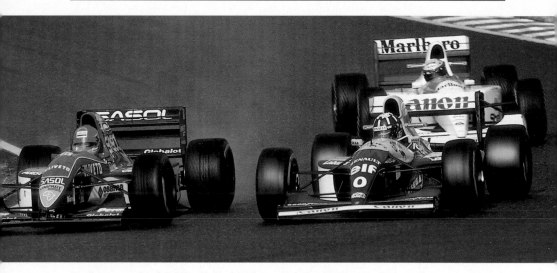

Reckless rookie? Eddie dives inside a slickshod Hill as a furious Senna looks on. (Autosport)

Eddie and Rubens Barrichello were not always the closest team-mates in the paddock . . . (Formula One Pictures)

Eddie had some storming drives for Jordan, but earned few solid results. This is Estoril 1994. (Formula One Pictures)

So close and yet . . . Jeff Krosnoff, Eddie and Mauro Martini ponder their disappointing second place at Le Mans in 1994. (Autosport)

Magny-Cours, 1994: Eddie Jordan reminds his friends at Ferrari of the latest World Cup news. (Formula One Pictures)

The 1995 car had plenty of power, but Eddie rarely saw the flag. (Peugeot)

Podium at last! Barrichello and Irvine celebrate their 2–3 finish at Montreal in 1995. (Peugeot)

Marriage made in heaven? New team-mates Irvine and Schumacher discuss life at Ferrari. (Formula One Pictures)

Left *Something new. Eddie tries his hand at snowboarding in early 1996.* (Pan Images)

Above *Good start! Eddie joined Hill and Villeneuve on the podium in Melbourne.* (Formula One Pictures)

Below *A nudge from Olivier Panis sent Eddie off the road at the Nurburgring.* (Empics)

Left *Eddie always has time for fans, but there are limits. He was mobbed at Imola after finishing fourth.* (Empics)

Above *Eddie at the wheel of his beloved Ferrari 288GTO, bought in 1993.* (Pan Images)

Below *For ever an Irishman! Eddie off duty at his local bar in Dalkey with a pint of Murphy's.* (Pan Images)

Eddie did a lot of waiting around in 1996. (Formula One Pictures)

Kathleen and Ed Sr — Eddie's number one fans. (Author)

attend the test, and by all accounts it was pretty meaningless.

'He was treated badly by the people that ran the test and might as well not have gone really. He got the short end of the stick, which was a shame. There was a fair amount of feeling within the team, as it was then, that tests shouldn't be taking place and they had better things to do, but they were contractually committed to it by Philip Morris.'

At the time, Eddie tried to be diplomatic, hoping that he might get further opportunities.

'I had some gearchange problems which weren't helped by me being long in the body. Getting second was a particular problem and I had to be early on the brakes to get all the shifting sorted out. On the positive side I enjoyed it, I learned Ricard, and it was far easier to drive than an F3000 car. Now I know there's no big deal about F1.'

That innocent last line, quoted in *Autosport*, went down like a lead balloon with Hunt, who by coincidence had tested a Williams at Ricard that very week as a PR exercise. It was uncannily reminiscent of a cocky remark made by countryman Tommy Byrne when he tested a McLaren in 1982, and which effectively finished the Ulsterman's F1 career before it started.

'It's the only time I ever saw Eddie criticised heavily by James Hunt,' says Mark Gallagher, then a journalist and Marlboro PR man. 'Hunt, Bogle, Mike Earle and co were very unimpressed. Hunt said, "it was bloody easy for him to say that when he's driven the car around a few seconds off a decent lap time, anybody can do that — it's when he has to get it down to running within a couple of tenths of where it ought to be, that's when we'll see if he's any good or not." That's where Hunt felt Eddie had overstepped the mark. People always felt that was a danger, but he always came back from the edge.'

A subsequent trip to the Onyx factory did not lead to an offer of further testing — instead he was apparently reprimanded for damaging the gearbox. Only later would Eddie confirm that the test had been a waste of time, he'd felt unwanted by team members who were Lehto fans, and JJ had blamed him for breaking the gearbox. Eddie gave his view on the subject in 1993, just three months before he linked up with Jordan: 'I didn't know the circuit, and I didn't know the car. The team didn't want me there because I was Mike Earle's man, and he'd just left the team. JJ definitely didn't want me there. Although my time didn't look good, Johansson went out straight after me and it took him seven laps to beat my time. I wish I hadn't done it, to tell you the truth. But at that stage I was in no control over my career, I just had to accept anything that was going. I felt completely powerless and I was wet behind the ears'.

The experience would be almost banished from his memory, and little

Left *The 1990 season saw a fresh start as Eddie joined Jordan and Camel.* (Autosport)

wonder that in seasons to come he would display a somewhat jaundiced view of F1. Three years and 10 months would pass before he next sat in a Grand Prix car.

Ironically, by the time the F1 test took place Eddie had already left the Marlboro family for pastures new. For 1990, Marlboro decided to switch its support from Pacific to the French DAMS team, which would run Comas and McNish. This time, there was nowhere for Eddie to go.

'I think that the tests that we did pointed towards the possible emergence of other talents,' says Bogle. 'We took a decision that we couldn't do another year with Irvine. One of the problems of that structure is that you are generating and promoting talent, and some individuals may not be able to progress year on year. It was a difficult decision to take, but we took it.'

Bogle offered to help Eddie find an alternative home, but the Irishman had plans of his own. He switched camps and joined Eddie Jordan Racing, in the process becoming a Camel-backed driver.

'I wouldn't have thought Graham was happy with that from a commercial point of view,' says Gallagher. 'But from a personal point of view he and Hunt and the little clique that supported Irvine were probably happy that he was continuing, and probably had their eye to get him back when they could.'

The two Eddies had been in contact on and off since 1985. Dubliner Jordan was intensely proud of his Irishness, and had taken great delight in promoting the career of Donnelly who, like Irvine, was from up north — but Irish all the same. His interest in Donnelly was not entirely patriotic, however, and extended to a lucrative management deal, as it did with Alesi and a host of other drivers who passed through EJ's hands.

For 1990, EJ had placed Alesi and Donnelly at Tyrrell and Lotus. He thus had plum vacant seats in his Camel-backed F3000 cars; the only hitch was that drivers had to generate their own funds to back up the Camel budget. It was a bit like the Duckhams Van Diemen arrangement of three years earlier, but on a somewhat grander scale. Nevertheless, from Irvine's point of view, joining EJR made sense. Herbert, Alesi and Donnelly had each used EJR as a stepping stone to Formula 1.

'I had to concentrate on getting myself in the best seat available to me,' he explained at the time. 'Eddie Jordan made me the offer and I'm happy to join the team. I need a manager as well, so that was another point in Eddie's favour. The money and sponsorship side is down to him.'

This time there was an extra carrot. A month after Eddie signed, EJ announced to the world that in 1991 he intended to step up to Grand Prix

The gang's all here. Frentzen, Naspetti and Irvine with EJ and his team.
(Autosport)

Eddie scored his first F3000 win with EJR. (Formula One Pictures)

racing in his own right. It was only logical to assume that a good season in F3000 might lead straight to a seat in his new F1 team. Three young men would be vying for that opportunity, for Irvine was joined at EJR by Emanuele Naspetti and Heinz-Harald Frentzen. The latter had strong support from Camel Germany, and was also a part of the new Mercedes junior sportscar team, alongside Schumacher and Karl Wendlinger. Yet again Eddie had the chance to challenge some reputations.

For various reasons, the season didn't go as planned. Running three cars was a little ambitious, never mind the fact that resources — financial and otherwise — were being pumped into the fledgling F1 programme. In addition, that year Lola had a real edge on the Reynard. For EJR, the writing was on the wall at the first race at Donington, when a poor fuel supply created misfires and Frentzen qualified eighth, Eddie 15th and Naspetti 17th. In the race all three ended up off the road, but only after Eddie had made an optimistic start and jumped up to fourth.

'He wasn't that happy at Jordan early on,' says Malcolm Oastler. 'I was still quite close to him and he used to come round and tell me all his troubles.'

There was a long gap until the second race, but Eddie filled in one empty weekend by jetting off to Japan to take part in a 1000kms sportscar race at Fuji. Team owner Vern Schuppan wanted some young drivers for his Porsche 962s and Jordan was only too happy to supply them. Eddie was due to share with Johnny Herbert and Rickard Rydell, but didn't think much of the car in practice, when he posted his first laps in anything other than a single-seater. Torrential rain meant the race itself was cancelled, although BTCC ace Will Hoy recalls that at the drivers' briefing Irvine was keener than the experienced locals to get out and race. Still, he enjoyed the trip and took note of the big money which seemed to be swilling around the Japanese scene.

When the F3000 series resumed Eddie finished sixth at Silverstone, crashed with Fabrizio Barbazza at Pau, and non-started at Jerez after eating a dodgy burger. As in 1989, the season seemed to be falling apart. Trevor Foster, Eddie's engineer at Jordan, had faith in him however:

'The first impressions were that he was very quick. But I felt frustrated from my own side because he never quite applied himself. I always felt he had a lot of natural speed, but if he applied himself a bit more he would be more consistent and more of a complete racing driver. Although he drove some very good races for us, he struggled to be consistent, and that's purely because I think his discipline wasn't strong enough. By that I mean discipline on the track. Trying to get him to do a debrief was tough. We'd say "where are you braking", and he's say, "I'm not quite sure", and therefore when you need to repeat it, sometimes it was difficult.

'For sure he was very, very strong in a race. Wherever he qualified, you always knew that he would come round at least a place ahead of that. He was a very good starter, and a good instinctive racer. Unfortunately by then the Reynard was a second class citizen compared to the Lola, which became more apparent as the season went on. Heinz-Harald never really came to terms with the car at all. He was far too aggressive with it.'

At Monza Eddie fought back with a fine second place, right behind series leader Comas, then followed up with a fourth after a hectic race at Enna. By now he was firmly in the driving seat at EJR, as neither Frentzen nor Naspetti had achieved very much.

'He drove a stunning race at Monza,' says Foster. 'He kept Comas under pressure the whole way and did a blinding job.'

That season Eddie stayed with Mark Gallagher in Oxfordshire, and despite being just a step away from F1, still made his living by selling cars.

'He was always pleading poverty to me,' says Gallagher, 'and I have to say that I kind of fell for it! Then I began to realise that there were cars dotted over various parts of the country, and at some stage he told me he had a Sierra Cosworth tucked away somewhere. We began adding up the value of these cars, and I think there was about 40 grands worth around the place. So I began to feel less sorry for him, and on top of that I was aware of the fact that he was earning a bit of money out of racing as well.'

Foster did not fall for it. 'He'd turn up at test days late with no petrol in his car and say he needed a gallon of fuel. I'd tell him to go and buy some.'

Just getting to a test was an achievement. Gallagher recalls one famous occasion when the telephone rang in the middle of the morning.

'It was Trevor Foster at Donington saying "have you any idea where Irvine is — we've got three cars here which need various things bedding in, and he's supposed to be driving all three". I went upstairs only to find that he was in his room fast asleep! He says, "tell Trevor I'm not here". Five minutes later he re-appears with all his gear, and phones Trevor and pretends that he's actually left for Donington some time previously, has broken down, and was now getting going having fixed the car at the side of the road. Then he went shooting off in this battered old Mk3 Escort. It was slightly indicative of his approach to things . . .'

In a racing car, he was more organised. Eddie's big day came on a sunny Saturday in late July, at the race supporting the German GP. Damon Hill had been setting the pace and took pole, but on only the second lap spun off at the exit from the first corner. Eddie sailed into the lead and, successfully withstanding mid-race pressure from Marco Apicella, came home in front. Apart from his heat win at Macau in 1988, it was his first outright success since the Van Diemen days: 'I don't know whether I could have beaten Hill or not, but I didn't have to!'

'I gave him one of my best victories,' rues Damon today. 'He was up and down like a lot of people in 3000. There were opportunities, and other times when things didn't go that well.'

Confidence high, Eddie then took pole at Brands, his favourite track. Right alongside him was Hill. Six years earlier they'd shared a row in the Festival final, and this time Damon repaid the compliment by chopping across in front of Eddie at the wet start. Late in the race Eddie got back in front, but on a drying track a puncture, spin and tyre stop dropped him back to an eventual third. Still, it was further proof of his pace. At this point Eddie still had a chance of overhauling Comas for the title, but his season fizzled out with a huge crash with Barbazza in Birmingham, a third at Le Mans, and another collision at Nogaro. The outcome was third place in the championship behind Comas and van de Poele.

I knew there was no way I could get into F1 without money, and I didn't have any

Even before the end of the season, Comas had already secured a two-year Ligier deal. He was not the only F3000 driver with F1 aspirations. McNish had been testing for McLaren all season, van de Poele had been doing likewise for the new Lamborghini team, and Gianni Morbidelli was all set to do the upcoming Japanese and Australian GPs with Minardi. Eddie's hopes for 1991 lay solely with the Jordan team, and having seen off both Frentzen and Naspetti, he thought his chances good. But when it became apparent that EJ did not have a major sponsor and any drivers were expected to bring a substantial budget, Irvine knew he was wasting his time: 'I realised at this stage that there was just no point. I'd wised up, I knew that there was no way I was getting in there without money, I didn't have any, and there was no way I was getting any'.

Meanwhile, in November Eddie returned to Marlboro colours when he went back to Macau for a third crack with Dick Bennetts and West Surrey Racing, as partner to Mika Hakkinen. The Finn shared the front row with German F3 champion Schumacher, while Eddie lined up fourth, a good showing from a driver making the difficult step back to F3. Hakkinen threw away victory with a second heat crash, leaving Michael to head home Mika Salo and Eddie. After the usual Macau partying the F3 teams headed to Japan for a new event at Fuji, which was also won by Schumacher.

'Eddie loved it,' recalls Bennetts. 'He was ninth on lap 1, dropped back to 11th or 12th, then he came through to finish third. He was over the moon, and said he'd really enjoyed it because he'd passed so many cars. He

Macau 1990. Salo and Irvine with winner Schumacher, all looking fairly underwhelmed by their success. (PR Plus)

loved the old straight at Fuji and the slipstreaming and battling under braking.'

While Irvine was on his Far East trip Jordan unveiled its new F1 contender at Silverstone, and shortly afterwards announced that Bertrand Gachot was to drive it. Days later Hakkinen signed for Lotus. Eddie didn't seem to be on any F1 team's shopping lists, but he already had other plans. In the paddock at Fuji were several representatives of leading Japanese F3000 teams, looking around for drivers for 1991. Having won a race in Europe, and finished third in the points, E Irvine was obviously of great interest.

'I saw people talking to him,' says Bennetts. 'I should have asked for a commission on that. It all kicked off from that Fuji race . . .'

• CHAPTER FIVE •

Starting a new life

IN DECEMBER 1990 Eddie left Fuji convinced that his future lay in Japan. Foreigners, or 'gai-jins', had been racing there regularly since around 1983–4, when pioneers Geoff Lees, Stefan Johansson, Eje Elgh and Kenny Acheson first took on the local stars. Through that decade interest in motorsport soared. Honda took over F1, and as the economic 'bubble' inflated, so sponsors poured into both Grand Prix racing and the domestic F3000 series. By 1990 every major F1 team — including Ferrari — had at least one Japanese backer, and several had Japanese owners.

F3000 was driven largely by tyre companies Bridgestone, Dunlop and Yokohama, who financed endless days of testing. As the series grew, so did demand for talented imported drivers, since there was a limited number of suitably qualified locals. Wages were good because many European hotshoes turned their noses up at the chance, feeling that once in Japan they would be typecast and unable to return — even though Johansson, Thierry Boutsen, Emanuele Pirro and Ivan Capelli had all managed to get back to F1.

Long-term career moves were the last thing on Eddie's mind. The big cigarette sponsors had pulled out of European F3000, and he had no interest in finding his own budget. A third year in the series, with a host of young drivers coming up, was in any case unattractive. And F1, with or without Jordan, was a non-starter. In Japan he could be paid the sort of salary he'd previously only dreamed about, and that was a priority.

'At that stage it seemed like it was a fairly big leap away from where it was all happening in Europe,' says Mark Gallagher, 'but Eddie said the money was so bloody good. It was too good an opportunity to miss — he'd earn some money and retire. He said there was no point in doing F1,

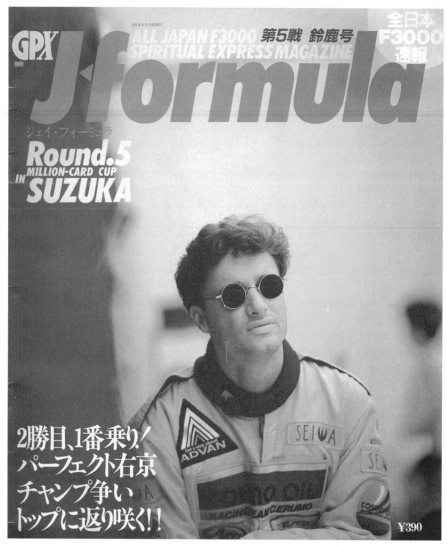

Cover boy! Eddie soon proved popular with the Japanese public.

because you'd need to bring shedloads of money, and the only point would
be if you were driving for a decent team, and that's not going to happen
overnight.

'He didn't appear to care a great deal about what would happen to him
once he'd been over there and earned a bit of money. I said to him, "what
would you do if you packed it in?" He said, "earn enough money to be

happy and go back to Ireland and sell cars". I was staggered he was saying it, and I wasn't sure whether to believe him or not, but felt he was probably being honest.'

Eddie had another reason to head to the Far East. His girlfriend of the time, Maria Drummond, lived in Macau. Of mixed Scots, Portuguese and Chinese blood, she had visited Eddie in Europe during the 1990 season but did not want to give up her job in, of all places, the Macau tax office. If Eddie was racing in Japan, they could spend more time together.

A dozen teams employed gai-jins, but more by luck than judgement Eddie ended up with one of the very best. Cerumo Racing was an unfamiliar name even to others who had raced in Japan, because for many years it operated under the name Hoshino Racing, achieving great success. At the end of 1990 driver Kazuyoshi Hoshino decided to run his own team, so Cerumo came out of the closet to compete in its own right. Owner Masayuki Sato, also the team's highly respected engineer and technical guru, succeeded in attracting sponsorship from Cosmo Oil, Japan's second biggest oil company. Since most F3000 backers were real estate or loan companies which had grown on the back of the 'bubble', this blue-chip support was most welcome. And it gave Cerumo the chance to find a quick, young foreign driver.

Team manager Yuichi Murayama had himself raced in British FF1600 and kept an eye on the action in Europe. Eddie's performance at Fuji — plus apparent interest in Japan — made him the number one candidate.

'I spoke to four or five drivers at Fuji, including Mika Salo and Michael Schumacher,' says Murayama. 'He was interested, but he had to consult with Mercedes first! Having watched from the outside of the track, Eddie was the best among them, apart from Schumacher. I wasn't really sure if Eddie wanted to come or not, but he was very enthusiastic about racing in Japan. Also, we wanted to have a driver who had experienced F3000 in Europe, and very few had. We thought some of the other guys were quick in F3, like Otto Rensing and Laurent Aiello, but we had a bit of doubt because we knew that Japanese F3000 has got a lot more grip than European F3000, and it was an even bigger step from F3. So Eddie was the one.'

Lola's Nick Langley, who dealt with the Japanese teams and helped steer Eddie into the deal, agrees that Cerumo was a good choice.

'I couldn't say that we introduced Eddie to them, but for sure there was some correspondence between us and Murayama, telling them what Eddie was about. I think Sato was one of the best engineers in Japan. He was one of those back room boys, not high profile, who gets the job done.'

Supporters like James Hunt and Graham Bogle endorsed Eddie's decision.

'We always remained in touch,' says Bogle. 'He was able to command a

One man and his dog. Eddie had a lot of fans in Japan. (Author)

Eddie leads the field at Fuji Speedway. (Author)

good racing programme in Japan at a time when Europe was flat, and at a time when his sponsorship support could never finance a competitive drive in F3000 or F1. Japan was the key to him because he was able to accumulate an income, and he could look back into Europe and keep an eye on opportunities. And that is effectively what he did.'

'I think Hunt might have been an influence on him going to Japan,' says David Marren. 'Eddie needed to get some money. He could have stayed in Europe, but if he stayed and he didn't get the right drive, he could easily have taken the shine off his star.'

Despite his experience, Eddie had to find his feet and adjust to the peculiarities of the local scene. Not least among these was the tyre war. Effectively a new team, Cerumo could not get a plum Bridgestone deal and had to go with Yokohama, the least consistently competitive of the three tyre companies. At the heart of the tyre war were qualifiers, sticky specials good for literally a single flying lap, something Eddie had not come across in Europe. However, he'd always had a talent for pulling a quick time out of the hat, and it would serve him well here.

'With the qualifying tyres it was a question of having supreme confidence in the car and yourself,' says Langley. 'You didn't have time to find out if it was capable of doing it — you had to be able to barrel into the corners flat out.'

Eddie signed his deal before even stepping aboard the car, and his first test in the Lola-Mugen, at Suzuka in early 1991, came as a shock to the system.

'It was a bit funny, because Eddie rated the Japanese series lower than the European one,' says Murayama. 'And after he drove five laps, his neck went because of the high grip in the corners! But the comments he made were pretty accurate, so we were quite happy with his performance.'

In Japan, Eddie came across a few old friends and rivals. Starting his second year there was none other than Johnny Herbert, still trying to find his way back to F1 after being dropped by Benetton. Then there was Volker Weidler, a fellow Marlboro man who'd had a disastrous year in F1 with Rial, Paulo Carcasci and Roland Ratzenberger, old mates from the FF1600 days, and fellow newcomer Salo. Others in the field, some of whom he'd never met, included Lees, Ross Cheever, Thomas Danielsson, Maurizio Sandro Sala, Jan Lammers, Enrico Bertaggia, Mauro Martini and Jeff Krosnoff. In early 1991 there were as many as 37 cars at some races, and even making the field was an achievement.

Among the F3000 drivers, and the other group who raced only in sportscars or touring cars, there was a close camaraderie. They would travel to the races together. Fuji involved everyone piling into cars for the run from Tokyo, while Suzuka and Sugo were reached by bullet train, and

Autopolis and Mine by a short internal flight. In the evenings, most would end up in the same restaurants, such as La Campanella in the Suzuka Circuit Hotel, or Par Pasta, the tiny Italian place near Fuji which had but five stools and a long wait at the counter.

In downtown Tokyo they would stay in the President Hotel, long-time home to the gai-jins. They shared the use of a pair of battered old bicycles which nominally belonged to Elgh and Pirro, although the latter was no longer in Japan. The drivers would socialise together in nearby Roppongi, a buzzing area of restaurants, bars and clubs, including the popular Hard Rock Cafe and the Lexington Queen, a small club whose Japanese co-owner was a big racing fan. At night Roppongi was the centre of attention for foreigners in Japan, whether they be businessmen, airline staff, American military, or postgraduates spending a year or two teaching English. Or indeed pouting gai-jin models, of whom there were hundreds in Tokyo on three-month stints. Racing drivers fitted easily into this cosmopolitan crowd.

The sharp business brain was put to good use investing his Yen earnings

In his first year at least, Eddie did not really become part of the gang. The team put him in a hotel some way from the President, so he saw little of the others, and Roppongi would remain a mystery to him. And while most stayed in Japan during any four or five day breaks between races and tests, Eddie would head back to Macau to the flat he shared with Maria. This commute was not the work of a moment. It involved the hassle of a 90 minute bus or train ride to Tokyo's Nairita Airport, a four-hour flight to Hong Kong, a bus or taxi to the harbour, another 90-minute ride on the packed, uncomfortable jet foil to Macau itself (if a seat was available) and then a cab to the flat. Eddie always loved travelling — 'there's nothing I like better than going down to the airport, sitting around reading magazines, then getting on a 'plane, it's great!' — but this was hard work, especially in the hot and humid summer months.

He soon discovered that outside the November race weekend Macau is hardly a vibrant place. His days usually consisted of lazily using up the hours before Maria came home by renting videos or reading the English language *South China Morning Post* from cover to cover and back again. That at least gave him a chance to keep a close eye on the Far East financial markets. The sharp business brain which was hitherto exercised by selling Irish-registered Sierras to unsuspecting Kentish punters was now put to good use as he carefully invested his Yen earnings.

On the track, that first season was more than satisfactory, although

All-action Saturday night in the Par Pasta cafe near Fuji in 1992: Villeneuve (hidden), Eddie, Ratzenberger, a thinning Sandro Sala, Raphanel, Danielsson and Elgh enjoy the cuisine. (Author)

Eddie's form was directly related to that of his Yokohama tyres. He also had to get used to seeing the same circuits again and again; the series consisted of four races at Fuji, four at Suzuka and one each at Autopolis, Mine and Sugo.

The huge field was split into two for qualifying, and in the opening race at Suzuka Eddie qualified a respectable fifth in his half of the draw, and finished eighth in the race. Second time out at Autopolis he was top of his group, and finished fifth in the race. The fourth round at Mine was held in monsoon conditions, and Yokohama's wet tyres proved just the ticket. As most of the top runners fell off the road, Eddie splashed around to claim victory, although he was extremely lucky to recover from a spin of his own. That was followed by a fourth at Suzuka.

With 14 points notched up after five rounds Eddie was looking good, but the remaining five races brought no more top six finishes, usually because the tyres let him down. He certainly benefited from the thousands of testing miles he completed, however.

'I think it was good experience for him,' says Murayama. 'Although he struggled with what was not the best tyre, he learned how to develop the tyres, how to comment on the set-up of the chassis, things like that.'

The championship was won by Ukyo Katayama, who undoubtedly had the best package, while Eddie finished seventh. He was the best non-Bridgestone runner, and third best gai-jin behind series veterans Cheever and Weidler. He easily outscored Herbert, but at the end of the year Johnny headed back to Europe and a drive with Team Lotus, while Ukyo signed for Larrousse. Another name to make the crossover to F1 was Michael Schumacher. The Mercedes sportscar junior turned up for the Sugo race, finished second, and a month later made his sensational F1 debut at Spa for Jordan — in the very car that Eddie once thought he might drive.

That year Eddie did more than enough to retain the coveted Cerumo seat for 1992 — and command a much higher salary for his second season. His apparently casual approach to the job had not always gone down well in Europe, but funnily enough it was just what he needed in Japan. 'You have to have a different mind set to make it work over there,' says Nick Langley. 'They don't really like to take too much of a lead from what the driver tells them. They'll listen politely, but if you start insisting that they've got the wrong rear springs on the car, do this, do that, you're on a hiding to nothing, and I've seen several European drivers fail in that way. Eddie's approach was very much the laid back one. He didn't impose his set-up philosophy, and was happy to get in the car and drive whatever Sato gave him. They had a great deal of respect for him.'

Cerumo also ran an F3 car on behalf of TOM'S Toyota. In 1992 Eddie had a new junior team-mate in the shape of Jacques Villeneuve, who had just spent three years in the Italian series. Like Eddie, the young French-Canadian gained a lot from his spell in the Far East.

'It was a great team, and Sato was very good,' Villeneuve remembers. 'He was very useful for me experience-wise, because he had a lot of experience himself. Even though he didn't speak much English he still managed to make it work. I think Japan is a great school, both the F3 and F3000. You get much more mileage than you would in Europe, and in F3000 on qualifying tyres they were going very quickly.

'The level was fairly competitive. I think it was better to be there than to try to pay your way into racing in Europe and not get the mileage and not be ready for F1. I found Eddie a very nice guy, very open and outgoing. He was friendly right away — it was very easy to get along with him.'

During 1992 Eddie had a brief attempt at making a more permanent base in Japan. The team loaned him a tiny apartment in Gotemba, not far from Fuji, where Cerumo and many of the other teams were located. At the start of the season Maria came over from Macau with him, but she soon christened the place 'Hell'. After a couple of weeks she returned home and waited for Eddie to resume his commuting.

Eddie undertook a serious physical training regime in Japan. (Author)

Bad hair day. The hazards of a windswept Fuji . . . (Author)

97

Overlooking a bowling alley carpark, Hell had two small, grubby rooms, although Eddie only really used one — the second had no light or furniture. But then the first had only a TV, a mattress and assorted blankets! The old-style Japanese bath, in which one squatted rather than reclined, had to be filled with cold water which was then heated by the adjacent boiler. After around 40 minutes the water at the top would be piping hot, while down below it was still freezing. Since there was very little worth stealing, Eddie wouldn't bother to lock the gates of Hell when he went out. Even when he went back to Europe.

At night about the only places in Gotemba worth visiting were McDonalds and the nearby newsagent, where Eddie would flick through the car magazines. Sometimes he'd go fishing or play a bit of golf, and since a round cost a fortune he would sneak on and play as many holes as possible before being chased away. At least he wasn't on his own in Gotemba, as F3 drivers Tom Kristensen and Rickard Rydell lived across town. Eddie also had an old Toyota Supra on loan from the team, in which a Thin Lizzy concert tape ran almost permanently. He would occasionally make forays into Tokyo, an hour and a bit up the motorway. This was when Eddie first properly discovered Roppongi. One visit, with Kristensen and Rydell on board, proved particularly memorable.

'The first time I really met him was when we went into Tokyo together,' recalls Kristensen. 'We went to the Lexington Queen and we were there all night. I had the car keys because I'd lost the bet and was driving, and when we went to leave, someone had stolen my jacket — and the keys — from the locker. The others were not really impressed! The parking was of course very much illegal, it was 5am, and we were very knackered. So we headed off to the President Hotel . . .'

Mauro Martini remembers the night well: 'They checked the room numbers of the drivers; I was there, Jeff Krosnoff was there and Marco Apicella was there, and they all went to different rooms. At 5am I was woken up, and Eddie just came in. He didn't say, "hey Mauro, I lost the key". He just came in, jumped in the bed and started to sleep. I didn't know what was going on. "What's this, what are you doing?" He wasn't really speaking — he mumbled something about keys. In the end I gave him a pillow and he slept on the floor. At 8am I woke up and thought, "was it a nightmare — was it really Eddie last night?" I looked around the room and couldn't see him.

'Then all of a sudden he sat up, and there was his face at the end of the bed. "What time is it, what time is it?" "It's 8am." "OK". And he went to sleep again. I went downstairs, had breakfast, and went upstairs again at 10am. He was making international phone calls from my room! But it's hard to get pissed off with him. That's just Eddie.'

Eddie and Roland Ratzenberger egged each other on in the SARD Toyota.
(Author)

Hell was soon abandoned, and Eddie joined the others as a regular guest of the President Hotel. Spending more time in Tokyo between races gave him plenty of opportunities to frequent Roppongi's colourful nightspots. Like any Irishman he liked a convivial bar atmosphere, and his regular haunt was Motown, a small up-the-stairs place where soul music and his beloved Van Morrison played round-the-clock.

Eddie had a more consistently competitive second season, as the team switched from Yokohama to Dunlop rubber. Bridgestones were still regarded as the thing to have, but as one of Dunlop's top drivers Eddie had an advantage some days. He had also learned from his first season: 'It's the first time I've ever been with a team for more than one year. They understand what you want from a car, and I know their little idiosyncracies. It's so much better.'

Now used to the all-or-nothing one lap qualifying routine, he regularly started from the front row. In the second round at Fuji he qualified second, but finished only fourth when clutch problems saw him get away badly.

'The problem that year was the reliability of the gearbox and clutch,' says Murayama. 'It was the first year that we fitted a carbon clutch, which made things difficult for us and for Eddie as well. It took some time for us to get 100% used to it. Also, we had to develop the tyres with Dunlop.'

In the third F3000 race at Mine, scene of his wet weather triumph the previous year, Eddie took his first Japanese pole. He made a good start and led all the way, surviving strong pressure from Martini and Ratzenberger, and ended the day as championship leader.

In the early races Cerumo had run a second car for Rydell, but next time out at Suzuka the Swede was replaced by 1990 champion Hitoshi Ogawa, who had been away racing for TOM'S Toyota in the World Sportscar Championship. Although already aged 36, Ogawa was being groomed for the TOM'S F1 team, which was slowly taking shape in Britain under the guidance of John Barnard. Eddie was keeping an eye on this project as it might represent a future opportunity to break into F1.

He was straightforward and said what he thought — sometimes it wasn't comfortable

---

That weekend the Irishman qualified second, but first gear broke at the start, and he was rammed from behind. Meanwhile Ogawa's first single-seater outing of the year ended in tragedy when he collided with Andrew Gilbert-Scott as the pair battled for fourth. He was launched high into the air and suffered a massive, fatal impact with a heavy fence post at the first corner. His family lived locally and as is Japanese custom the funeral ceremonies started that same night. A shocked Eddie was asked by the Cerumo team to check out of the Suzuka hotel and join the mourners. The accident took the momentum out of the TOM'S F1 project, and with finance short, it was eventually abandoned. Barnard joined Ferrari as Director of Research and Development.

With the Japanese F3000 series enjoying a long summer break, Eddie's next race was to be his first in Europe for 20 months — and his debut at the Le Mans 24 Hours. SARD Toyota had long been the home of Roland Ratzenberger, who had become a strong influence within the team and often seemed to call the shots. In the Japanese sportscar series he was partnered by Swedish veteran Elgh. Eddie was hired as third driver at Le Mans, and as a taster he had joined the squad for a 1000kms event at Fuji in early May.

Eddie had long been used to outrunning team-mates, but taking on someone in the same car was a novelty. Typically he just turned up and nonchalantly matched Roland's pace, and cared little for the Austrian's apparent seniority within the SARD set-up. Elgh watched developments with some interest:

'Initially I thought Eddie was rather cocky, but he was very friendly and had a laid back attitude which I took a liking to. It was like a positive cockiness — it wasn't like he was bullshitting. He was very, very straightforward and said what he thought, and sometimes it wasn't comfortable for everyone. I knew that he was quick in F3000, and in sportscars he was very quick straight away. It made Roland a total wreck. I thought I had a good relationship with Roland, and it basically turned to shit once Eddie got in, because Roland was very nervous about the whole thing. Obviously he thought his position was threatened — which it was!

'In fact it took me a while to accept his speed. I thought it was one thing to do a quick lap, but it's another to do a full stint of an hour, once you get tired and the track gets dirty. But he coped too bloody well with it! You always want to be competitive and it's hard to accept that anyone is quicker. Eddie was the first guy that made me run out of excuses for myself. He was a far better driver than I was and it was something I just had to accept'.

The Fuji weekend started disastrously when Roland had a huge crash while gunning for pole position; a case of trying too hard. The repaired car ran well in the race until the gearbox failed. The trio stayed together for Le Mans in June. Roland had always loved the event and Eddie was enthralled from his first laps of the place. They spurred each other on, and Elgh, who was on the verge of retiring anyway, had no wish to try to outpace the two young guys. When he moderated his pace during a night-time session of rain and fog, Roland became frustrated as the car lost time. Eddie in turn took Eje's side.

'There was a lot of tension there,' recalls Elgh. 'Ideally three drivers is the thing to have at Le Mans, but it's got to be three drivers who can work together and be close to each other. That combination of drivers wasn't all that good, and one of them had to suffer — and at that time it was me. It didn't really matter as it was nearly the last race I did anyway. But for me it proved that Eddie was a good man. He did a very good job, and the thing is he did it without adding all the crap and bullshit to prove that he is good, unlike many other people. Eddie proved it with lap times.'

The car ran sixth at halfway, leading the turbo class behind the works Peugeots and Toyotas, but after clutch problems and an early morning gearbox change it was demoted to a distant ninth. Still, Eddie had enjoyed the circuit and vowed to come back.

The F3000 series resumed at Autopolis in late July. With Saturday qualifying fogged off, Eddie took another pole on race morning. Yet again, the transmission gremlins returned; this time first *and* second gears broke on the line!

'Exactly the same as Suzuka,' he complained. 'Nine points down the tubes.'

The Dunlops faded away during the hot summer months, and Eddie never quite regained his stunning early season form. Indeed, after the Mine win and a string of retirements he added just a fourth and fifth place to his tally. Meanwhile a new face in Japan was his former EJR F3000 team-mate Heinz-Harald Frentzen, who had been plucked from the scrapheap to replace points leader Volker Weidler, sadly sidelined by a hearing problem.

Over in Europe the troubled World Sportscar Championship had come to an end, and in Japan too the local series was on the verge of folding. At the final race at Mine in November Toyota entered a pair of its TS010 cars by way of a swansong, the first driven by regulars Lees and Lammers and the second by a one-off junior squad, comprising Eddie and F3 drivers Villeneuve and Kristensen. Eddie really got to grips with the car, which with its high downforce and 3.5-litre normally aspirated engine was nothing less than a two-seater F1 machine, and made the turbo car he'd driven at Le Mans seem like a truck. Naturally, all three young drivers were keen to make an impression, although Jacques says he wasn't out to beat Eddie.

Eddie shares an after dinner joke with Marco Apicella, fellow future Jordan F1 driver. (Author)

'I wouldn't say we were rivals,' recalls Villeneuve. 'First of all, he was the experienced guy in there anyway. All I wanted to do was learn. We ended up quite a good team, wanting to make it work. Once we got to the race we weren't trying to be quicker than each other just because that was important. He didn't seem to be too concerned about beating his team-mates.'

The race was a frantic wet and dry affair, and the 'juniors' brought the car home fourth overall, the star of the event having been Nissan driver Frentzen.

'We went very well,' recalls Kristensen, 'and I was very close to Eddie's times. But he was very quick to point out that second gear broke when I was driving! Jacques and me came from F3, and we wanted to look good, not be too slow but not make too many mistakes, while Eddie was there to prove himself and beat Lammers and Lees.'

Jacques says: 'It was a great experience and we had a great time, but I was a little bit out of my depth at that point as I was just out of F3. We finished the race with a few gears missing, but all in all we had a pretty good result'.

The F3000 finale at Suzuka a fortnight later brought another disappointing retirement. Eddie finished the season in an unrepresentative eighth place, albeit only 18 points behind champion Mauro Martini. He signed a deal for a third year with Cerumo, and as usual he managed to increase his salary. He had no idea what the next 12 months would bring.

• CHAPTER SIX •

Too long
in exile

FOR EDDIE IRVINE, 1993 was to be a momentous year. First he gave himself a present — the Ferrari he'd always wanted. Not just any old Ferrari, but a classic 1984 288GTO which set him back over £200,000. The days of turning up at races in old Escorts and Fiestas were seemingly over. Not that Eddie got much chance to use his new toy, as it sat in England while he spent another season in Japan.

By 1993 former European F3000 rivals Marco Apicella and Emanuele Naspetti had joined the series, and they fitted in perfectly with Eddie's sense of fun. 'Eddie was the best thing about Japan,' says Naspetti, who stayed for only a few races before heading back to Italy, unable to cope with the Eastern mentality.

With the Cerumo team sticking with its proven 1992 Lola, and the clutch problems a thing of the past, Eddie was competitive from the off. He started the year with third places at Suzuka and Fuji, although on both occasions the Dunlop runners were outclassed. He then went to Mine looking for a hat trick at the twisty track. He took pole, but as in 1991 the race was held in monsoon conditions. After a chaotic re-start Eddie was running well in second place when he was hit by Heinz-Harald Frentzen as they entered the pit straight. Eddie was out of the race, and to this day holds it against the German! Some sort of recompense was gained at Suzuka two weeks later when he took another pole and, under strong pressure from Toshio Suzuki, scored his first win of the season. It was his third success since coming to Japan, and further proof of his strong form.

'I'd say he was a very, very good natural driver,' says Yuichi Murayama. 'Quick over one lap, but also very strong in the races. He kept on saying that he didn't have to be one lap ahead of the guy behind, but maybe a tenth could still make you win. At Suzuka he was holding Suzuki up from the start to the end, which gave me the impression he was clever, and knew how to hold people back.'

After Suzuka there was a 10-week break in the F3000 series, but in the middle of it Eddie had a commitment at Le Mans. Once again he was to drive a Toyota, but this time it was to be the works, normally-aspirated TOM'S car he'd raced at Mine. Unlike the SARD turbo car, it would give him a serious chance of victory, since only 1992 winners Peugeot stood in Toyota's way. This would be the final fling for the 3.5-litre atmo cars; a classic contest was in prospect, and Eddie was well aware that he had a chance to create some headlines.

The week of the race started off with some sad news. On Tuesday morning James Hunt died in his sleep in London, and I broke the news to Eddie and the other drivers that evening.

'Hunt took a very, very close interest in everything that Irvine was doing,' says Philip Morris's David Marren. 'Even though Irvine wouldn't call him very often from Japan, the odd time he did call, Hunt made it his business to find out what he was up to out there. There was a great belief in Irvine, and a feeling that if he didn't make it, this would be a great loss to motorsport.'

Eddie had no idea that he would walk away from Japanese F3000. This was a practice mishap at Suzuka. (Author)

At Le Mans, after his impressive testing performances Eddie was given Toyota's sole qualifying engine on Thursday evening, but his first flying lap ended with a gentle spin into the gravel at Mulsanne corner. Despite traffic, he was heading for a time seven seconds quicker than Philippe Alliot's pole! The car was cleaned up and readied for another run, but Toyota's conservative management decided not to allow Eddie out again, much to his frustration.

Saturday also started badly for Eddie, when in the warm-up he clipped the private Ferrari 348 of Robin Smith, sending it into the wall. Once the race got under way he soon relieved Alliot of the lead and led strongly for the first couple of stints. But co-drivers Toshio Suzuki and Masanori Sekiya couldn't match his pace, and throughout the race Eddie would continue to make up ground lost by his partners, or by the team in the pits. Still, the car hung on to third place until it needed a transmission change on Sunday morning. Peugeot scored a stunning 1–2–3, a fitting end to Jean Todt's tenure as the marque's competitions chief before he moved to Ferrari as Sporting Director. Irvine and co eventually finished fourth, Eddie having set a lap record which will never be beaten, since rule changes mean that sportscars will never be as quick as they were in 1993.

Among the visitors to Le Mans was none other than Eddie Jordan, now halfway through his team's third season in F1. Jordan GP was having mixed fortunes: new boy Rubens Barrichello impressed, but Ferrari dropout Ivan Capelli had been a disappointment. He was replaced by Thierry Boutsen who was hardly more competitive and, like Capelli, was completely over-shadowed by the young Brazilian. There were already rumours that he would retire before the end of the year, and that his seat would be available.

The two Eddies met and talked over old times. It amounted to a thawing of their relationship, which had not been especially close since Irvine went to Japan at a time when EJ was still, officially, his manager.

'I think you only ever fall out with Eddie or with me if it involves money,' smiles Jordan today. 'To say there was a falling out is not really a correct statement; absent-mindedness on his part, perhaps, or a forgetting of the reality. Something conveniently dissipated out of his mind! He was set up, he was making his money, he was very content there. And with respect, he didn't need me. So therefore there was little or no communication.

'But you can't shake somebody like Irvine out of your mind. He has an uncanny ability to suck people to his side, and change things. You either love him or you hate him, and there's no ground in the middle, as far as I can see. I'm one of the people he has touched, for want of a better word! I think Le Mans was when F1 really came up again. We patched up our misunderstandings from previous years, although patched up is a very generous word.'

Toshio Suzuki dives inside Eddie at Mine. Later on he was pushed off by Frentzen. (Author)

The week after Le Mans Eddie voiced his own assessment of the situation:
'Japan is either a way of me getting a good position in F1, or it's a good career for me in itself. If F1 doesn't materialise I'm in a position where I can win races every weekend, I get paid good money, I'm with the team I want to be with. I would like to get to F1 but I don't want to get there with a shitty team. Most of the guys want to be in F1 just for the sake of it, and I don't want that. Luckily enough I don't have to do that. You need to be like Schumacher — get in the right car at the right time and do the right job. But that's more luck than judgement'.

After Le Mans Irvine stayed some time in England, and went to the British GP where he spent much of the weekend hanging around the Jordan motorhome.

'We kept in touch,' EJ recalls. 'He was always making it clear that paying for drives in F1 wasn't his bag. He didn't have a goldmine behind him, he was a young Irish guy without money, he needed to earn money to stay alive, and in Japan he was away from the mumbo jumbo of Europe, with people going around selling themselves. Eddie had never been one to sell himself on a commercial basis, and in many respects still isn't, and he is very happy and comfortable with that.'

The following week Eddie headed back to Japan by way of Toronto, where he visited relatives and had his first look at the IndyCar scene. Toyota was planning an entry into the series, and joining their programme seemed like a possibility some years down the line. Using a pass borrowed from Stefan Johansson he mooched around the paddock for a couple of days, said hello to Villeneuve (now racing in the Atlantic series), and made a half hearted effort to introduce himself to a few IndyCar team VIPs. Their total lack of recognition of the new Le Mans lap record holder was disappointing. Any thoughts of trying his luck in America were forgotten.

Back in Japan, Eddie's F3000 form was better than ever. At Sugo he was on pole again, and led for seven laps until a misfire intervened. After a pit stop, he trailed home a frustrated 15th.

'He had to come in because it was misfiring quite badly,' recalls Murayama. 'After the race as he stopped at the parc ferme he said to me "that's one way to lose the championship". It was a good and very bad prediction, but I didn't take it very seriously at the time.'

It was nice to have a decent bit of input from an up-and-coming driver

The next race at Fuji was abandoned when fog closed in after the warming up lap. Three weeks later on 5 September the series was back at Fuji, and again Eddie had a misfire, this time in qualifying. Starting 22nd, he charged up to sixth. After the race, one of the drivers had a particular reason to get back to Europe in a hurry; Marco Apicella was to make his F1 debut at Monza the following weekend for Jordan.

The beleagured Boutsen had, as expected, bowed out of F1 after the Belgian GP. With Italy, Portugal, Japan and Australia left on the schedule, Jordan and his commercial manager Ian Phillips had been juggling potential candidates around. Apicella came up with the money for Monza, but couldn't do Portugal as it clashed with a Suzuka race. So that went instead to his pal Naspetti, who had long since abandoned Japan in frustration and headed home. With Frentzen having recently made a trip to Mugello to test for Sauber, and Toshio Suzuki having agreed to drive for Larrousse in the last two GPs, there was suddenly a flow of drivers from Japan to F1.

Eddie intended to be next in line. The Jordan seat was still available for the last two GPs, and together with friend David Smith, a Japanese-American wheeler dealer who had arranged the Cosmo/Cerumo sponsorship, he was trying to raise the necessary funds. In Europe he had an ally in Marlboro's Graham Bogle who was lobbying on his behalf. After Cosmo agreed to provide the bulk of the cash, Irvine headed back to England to finalise the deal. Phillips, who had the job of tying up the loose ends, knew Eddie only by reputation.

'I'd heard about him and been vaguely introduced a couple of times, but I never really knew the guy until he came and sat down in front of me to do a contract! He'd phoned EJ, some time in August I think, and asked how much it would be to do the two races. There was an outstanding issue between them, from before my time, which had to be resolved, but it was sorted within the initial package.

'I don't think anybody really knew what to expect at all. There were a lot of people within Jordan who'd known him before, and there was no doubt about it, their anticipation was that he would be quick. There was a good PR side to it, the Irish side, but everybody said to me, "the man's a complete animal!" But within about 30 seconds of meeting him, I thought "this is my kind of guy."'

Jordan was perhaps the only team in the pit lane which, while sponsored by the South African Sasol concern, could simultaneously pull off a deal with a company called Cosmo Oil. The contract completed, and a seat fitting undertaken, Eddie then headed back for the next F3000 race at Suzuka on 26 September. On Sunday morning, Cosmo made a press announcement, and Eddie looked a little sheepish posing in a set of ex-Boutsen Jordan overalls.

Le Mans 1993. Eddie with Toyota team-mates Toshio Suzuki (left) and Masanori Sekiya. (Autosport)

In the race Eddie kept up his championship challenge with second place, then back in the President Hotel on Sunday night he watched Naspetti's one-off outing in Portugal end with *his* Jordan-Hart coasting to a halt with the engine in flames! Just two days later, Eddie climbed aboard the same chassis for a test at Estoril. It was his first run in an F1 car since that long forgotten Onyx outing at Paul Ricard in 1989, his first experience of the track, and his first time with both a semi-automatic gearbox and traction control. Jos Verstappen stole the headlines on his debut for Arrows, while Eddie finished the week a little slower than Barrichello. It was a steady but unspectacular debut.

'He was very spectacular at going into the gravel trap on a number of occasions!', says Phillips. 'He had an engine go after a few laps, then went off, then came on the 'phone to us and said it was the most appalling car he'd ever driven in his entire life. To be fair Tim Wright, who was engineering him, took to him pretty quickly. He felt at long last he was getting somebody who was not only tried but understood what he wanted from a car. Within a short space of time they worked pretty well together and got something out of the car which had perhaps been lurking there undiscovered. Rubens was the new kid on the block and he easily beat the myriad of team-mates we put with him, but he didn't know what was good or bad. He was just happy to be in F1.'

The experienced Wright had joined Jordan direct from Peugeot's sportscar project.

'I'd met Eddie briefly at Le Mans,' he recalls. 'At Estoril first impressions were that he was a bit over confident. But the more you get to know him, that's normal, it's just the way he comes over. It was quite nice to work with him. He wasn't at all pretentious. He told you what he thought, and just got on with it. But it was refreshing, having worked the rest of the season with Boutsen. The car wasn't that bad, because Barrichello always got it up there somewhere. But it was nice to have a decent bit of input from an up-and-coming driver.'

Eddie struggled to get used to the traction control and felt extremely uncomfortable in the cockpit.

'The big problem is that the car is so small,' he reported. 'I could only do about four laps at a time because my back got so sore. I'm bent over in the car, and I don't know what we can do. I did about 80 or 90 laps over the three days. I had a few spins, but it went quite well. The telemetry is great. It tells you exactly where you're losing out. Barrichello was quicker in the two hairpins; you see him standing on the power and letting the traction control do everything. It's very difficult to make your brain think like that!'

Eddie also explained his ambivalent attitude towards F1.

'I'm in a very strong position in Japan; I've got a very good sponsor, and a

Eddie leads the field away at Sugo in August 1993, with Frentzen tucked in behind. A misfire effectively cost him the title. (Author)

Smile please! Eddie relaxes at Suzuka with Jeff Krosnoff (left) and his future biographer. (Author)

good team. The racing here is very competitive, and I run at the front all the time. I don't want to get my arse into F1 just for the sake of being there! Whatever I'm driving, as long as I'm happy with the job I've done, that's all I care about. But obviously, to everybody else, if you're not in F1, you're a nobody.'

After the test he headed back to Japan for another F3000 race at Fuji on 17 October, in which he took pole and finished second. Veteran Hoshino won and took the points lead on 32, while Eddie had 30 and erstwhile leader Cheever 25. Just one race remained, but in the meantime Eddie had a couple of Grands Prix to get out of the way. On Tuesday Eddie met up with Damon Hill for lunch at the Hard Rock Cafe, before heading down to Suzuka and the weekend of his life.

'It always surprised me that, when he came into F1 and got the tag of being wild,' says Hill today. 'He wasn't wild in FF1600 or F3. He was very smooth and consistent, and he was "Steady Eddie" in those championships. He certainly had a dynamic entrance to F1.'

Eddie was in the news from the start of the weekend. At the end of the first unofficial session on Friday morning, the times read Hill, Hakkinen, Alesi, Schumacher — and Irvine. Mechanical troubles dropped Senna and Prost down the order, but local knowledge or not, it was an impressive performance. Problems in qualifying saw Eddie only 11th in the afternoon, but when it counted on Saturday, he moved up to eighth.

'We'd opted for this longer wheelbase configuration,' recalls Wright, 'and there were a couple of mods. He said, "yes it's magic", and hey presto he was up there with the big boys, which rocked the establishment a little bit. Having spoken to him about the place, he obviously knew the ins and outs of Suzuka and was going to come up with something, but I didn't expect it to be that good!'

Once again, Eddie had shaken a highly rated team-mate. To put this into perspective, you need to recall that at the time Barrichello was the next superstar, the logical successor to Senna. He'd destroyed Capelli and Boutsen, but only once, in France, did he qualify inside the top 10, and elsewhere the quicker Jordan was usually between 13th and 17th. He was undoubtedly revved up by Eddie's presence, and pulled out all the stops to take 12th — and promptly fell off the road. Suddenly, everyone took notice of Irvine.

'Suzuka was very special for him,' say Barrichello, 'and he was very impressive first time out in the car. Because it was my first time in Suzuka I was completely lost and I really felt the pressure. I had to learn how Eddie was, because he was different from anyone else.'

Right *The Grand Prix world meets E. Irvine — press conference at Suzuka.*
(Autosport)

The stunning qualifying performance was carried over to the race. On the grid, Eddie said that at the first corner he intended to take the outside line which, after eleven F3000 races in three years, he knew to be quick. It was. When the field came out of the second corner, the order was Senna, Prost, Hakkinen, Berger and Irvine. His aggressive tactics had taken him past Schumacher, Hill and Warwick!

'He had the start of the race planned,' says Wright. 'He had this thing from F3000 about going round the outside. He said the car would stand it. So that didn't come as any surprise.'

It took Michael a couple of laps to re-pass him, and it was another four before Damon made it by. After the German crashed into Hill and some of the top guys pitted for tyres Eddie rose once again to fourth place, at which point it started to rain. The slower pace came as a huge relief, because 'my back was in agony. After 10 laps I thought I couldn't take any more'.

Knowing how quickly the track could change, Eddie wanted to come straight in, but the team kept him out as it first wanted to service Barrichello, then running ninth. By the time Eddie was allowed in, the track was completely awash, and as he tiptoed round he lost great chunks of time. By a whole lap he was the last of the 20 cars still running to pit, and the damage had been done; he'd dropped to tenth, while Rubens rose to sixth.

Now even more inspired, Eddie drove flat out to regain time. Having risen to seventh, Eddie was catching Hill. At the same time, he was being followed by race leader Senna.

'He couldn't catch me, and then somebody put oil down at Degner. I just slid wide on it. I could have snapped back on the track, but I knew Senna was behind, so I stayed out wide, and let him overtake. I followed him for a couple of laps, but he was so bloody slow . . .'

Damon made a premature stop for slicks. Eddie knew that Suzuka took longer to dry out than most places. On wets, he still had an advantage. But, incredibly, Senna was in the way.

'I just had to get at Hill. So I had to overtake Senna, it was that simple. He seemed to be in a cautious mood, and I wasn't in a cautious mood! To be honest I didn't know he was leading the race, but I knew he was a lap ahead of me.'

Coming into the chicane, Eddie dived down the outside of a startled Senna, and set off after Hill. On the next lap he briefly passed Damon with a similar move, this time on the inside, but slid wide, and Damon got back in front. The same thing happened seconds later at the first corner. It was one of the most thrilling, wheel-to-wheel battles seen in years, but watching all this, and concerned about his lead over Prost, Senna was seething.

'It was great,' says Eddie. 'Hill was very slow in the corners, but he was very good on traction, so he was quick out of them. I was all over him but I couldn't get past, because I was too slow out of the corners. He was fair, and I think I was fair. Then I went off on the oil again. So Senna went past me again, and tried to hold me onto the dirt, which was fair enough as I shouldn't have been there! I pulled in behind him again, and we both went for slicks at the same time. It was the perfect time to do it, no question.'

The stop left Eddie in seventh, but he had his heart set on a point. He soon reeled in Warwick, who duly chopped him. On the penultimate lap he hit the Englishman in the rear at the chicane; both cars spun, but only Eddie got away. He claimed sixth place, leaving a fuming Warwick sitting at the trackside. Then on the last lap he had the temerity to unlap himself from a slowing Senna once again.

Senna headed for the Jordan camp to tell the upstart exactly what he felt

---

It had been an amazing 102 minutes for Eddie. He finished just 11 seconds behind fifth placed Barrichello, and the double helping of points was essential for Jordan, who had not scored all year. Eddie Jordan hugged both his drivers as they alighted from their cars, but Irvine's initial reaction was one of frustration and disappointment: he could have done so much more had he not been left out on slicks. But the scale of his achievement soon sank in. Everyone wanted to talk about the battle with Senna.

'He was quick all weekend,' says Jordan. 'If you actually think about it, I'm not sure he's had as good a drive since.'

'His start and the way he overtook people in the first couple of corners was pretty spectacular,' recalls Phillips. 'Irrespective of the rights or wrongs, and I'm still convinced that Eddie was 100% right in what he did, the over-riding feeling from a Jordan point of view was that we'd got a driver in the car who didn't give a stuff basically for anybody's name or reputation. He was in there to do a job, and it was total commitment. That was something we hadn't seen in a Jordan for a long time; since de Cesaris, to be honest.

'He got himself into a good position, and then fought like mad to hold on to it. It was great. Rubens had done a good job at Donington, but this was probably only the second time we'd seen a Jordan on TV all year! It was heartwarming after what had been a long, difficult and fairly dismal season.'

Irvine was called to see the stewards to discuss the Warwick incident; they accepted his straight-faced explanation that Derek had forced him off line, he'd got dirt on his tyres, and was thus unable to stop when the Footwork seemingly braked early for the chicane!

While EJ headed for the airport, Eddie, Rubens, Ian and a couple of

The famous battle with Hill at Suzuka. (Autosport)

other Jordan folk watched a replay of the race in the team's cabin behind the pits. A few yards away, in another cabin, Senna watched the same transmission. In the winner's press conference he'd slammed Eddie's driving, and as he watched the replay, with Gerhard Berger and others winding him up and — seldom a drinker — with schnapps generating a little fighting spirit, he resolved to do something about it. He headed for the Jordan camp to tell the young upstart exactly what he thought.

Having just finished interviewing Eddie, I switched my tape recorder back on and recorded the conversation for posterity. The next few minutes have passed into legend . . .

Senna's tone was, shall we say, aggressive. After a couple of minutes of discussion, this is how things developed:

Senna: 'I tell you something. If you don't behave properly in the next event, you can just rethink what you can do. I guarantee you that.'
Irvine: 'The stewards said no problem, nothing was wrong.'
Senna: 'Yeah? You wait 'til Australia, mate. You wait 'til Australia, and the stewards will talk to you. Then you tell me if they tell you this.'
Irvine: 'Hey, I'm out there to do the best I can for me.'

Senna: 'This is not correct. You want to do well. I understand, because I've been there, I understand. But it's very unprofessional. If you are a back-marker, because you are about to be lapped . . .'

Irvine: 'But I would have followed you if you had overtaken Hill!'

Senna: '. . . you should let the leader go by . . .'

Irvine: 'I understand that fully!'

Senna: '. . . and not come and do the things you did. You nearly hit Hill in front of me three times, because I saw, and I could have collected you and him as a result, and that's not the way to do that.'

Irvine: 'But I'm racing! I'm racing! You just happened to . . .'

Senna: 'You're not racing! You're driving like a ****ing idiot! You're not a racing driver, you're a ****ing idiot!

After that, there was no way back. Although Eddie didn't swear in return, he refused to concede that he'd done anything wrong. Senna was dumb-founded at the new boy's nonchalance. The debate finished like this:

Senna: 'You be careful guy.'

Irvine: 'I will, I'll watch out for you.'

Senna: 'You're going to have problems, not with me only, but with lots of other guys, and also the FIA.'

Alas, poor Warwick. After Eddie pushed him off Derek looked set to teach Eddie a lesson. Senna got there first. (Author)

Irvine: 'Yeah?'
Senna: 'You bet.'
Irvine: 'Yeah? Good.'
Senna: 'Yeah. It's good to know that.'
Irvine: 'See you out there.'
Senna: 'It's good to know that!'
Irvine: 'See you out there . . .'

At that point Senna, accompanied by three McLaren employees, turned to

Australia proved a huge anticlimax after the sensation in Japan. (Autosport)

leave the room. Had he done so, the whole thing might soon have been forgotten. But, a little tipsy and fuelled by Eddie's intransigence, he lashed out. Eddie leaned back and fell off the table on which he had been sitting, and Senna, still shouting, was dragged out of the room by his colleagues. News of the great punch-up spread round the paddock, and the press room, in minutes. And for the next 24 hours, Eddie was the second most famous racing driver in the world.

Not that Eddie realised what had happened. After Suzuka, he disappeared to Macau for a week, and was pretty much out of phone contact. When he arrived in Adelaide he was virtually mobbed by the media. Overnight he'd become a sought after commodity, and that weekend he

rubbed shoulders with such as George Harrison, Clive James and even Dame Edna Everage, although typically he was totally unimpressed.

On the track the weekend started well when he was quick in untimed practice, but he had problems in qualifying and started only 12th.

'Overall, yes, it was a huge disappointment,' says Phillips. 'Perhaps it wasn't to be unexpected. What impressed me was how Eddie learned the circuit very quickly. All right, at the end of the day Rubens outqualified him, but we had an electrical problem on the car. But he was in fact quicker than Rubens all the time except when it counted, which wasn't Eddie's fault. Of course he made a complete fool of himself on the grid.'

When he arrived at the start Eddie realised he was straddling the line marking his grid position. Rather than risk a jump start penalty — this was before the days of electronic detectors — he switched off the engine, waved to the marshals, and had the start aborted.

'He wasn't with the programme at all in Adelaide,' says Wright, who remembers the race with less enthusiam. 'He couldn't get to grips with the circuit. Admittedly we didn't do a good job with the car, and then he cocked up the start. He said he thought the best way out of it was to get the race stopped. He didn't realise that they'd put him at the back of the grid as a result! He thought he'd just get away with it. At that stage he got bored with it all, made a stupid error, locked up under braking and slid off. He wasn't getting anywhere anyway.'

'He defied all of the things I'd been saying about him,' rues Jordan. 'He was a hero one minute, then he didn't start in the right place, was put to the back of the grid, ran off the road and hit the wall in a very innocent looking accident. Everything that he did well in Japan, he did badly in Australia.'

There was another anticlimax to come. Eddie headed back to Japan for the Suzuka F3000 finale needing three points to dislodge Hoshino. However, on race morning someone pointed out that he'd have to drop his worst score — a sixth — which meant only third or better could do the job. Hoshino failed to score and Eddie finished fourth, to make the points scores 33:32 in his favour. The dropped sixth place made them equal, and Hoshino then took the title having won two races to Eddie's one. Frentzen's assault at Mine and the Sugo misfire suddenly seemed very expensive.

The season wasn't quite over however. Eddie had to head back to Paris for the FIA tribunal into the Senna affair, where my tape was 'Exhibit One'. He arrived straight off the 'plane in jeans, and although he was only called as a witness to Senna's indiscretion, the perceived lack of respect for the formal proceedings was frowned upon. Ayrton got away with a suspended ban, but on his next visit to Paris, Eddie himself would not be so lucky.

• CHAPTER SEVEN •

Even better than the real thing

EDDIE CAME BACK to Britain at the end of the 1993 season and spent the winter mostly at his sister Sonia's cottage in Kent. On the first Sunday of 1994, without anything better to do, he and I headed to Birmingham for the last day of Autosport International, the UK's leading motor racing show. He wandered around almost unrecognised by the public, but stopped to chat to a few familiar faces from his early days. Among them were Ralph Firman, John Uprichard and Malcolm 'Puddy' Pullen, who were manning the Van Diemen stand.

'He was in his Marlboro jacket and jeans,' recalls Uprichard. 'We were chatting away about life in Japan, and how he always wanted to get to F1 because the women were better! Right at the end of the conversation he produced this cheque.'

Seven years to the day since he got the works Van Diemen drive, Eddie had decided to pay off the balance of the £10,000 he owed Ralph Firman. Knowing nothing of his plan in advance, I stood there as surprised as the others.

'It's the best investment I ever made,' Eddie commented sheepishly, before wandering off.

'It was great,' says Ralph Firman, who chuckles at the memory. 'I might have said something like, "where's the interest" but I was delighted actually. There have been many drivers who've not paid their bills to Van Diemen — reasonably successful ones as well.'

'I always said that he would come and pay,' says Puddy. 'Ralph said, "no, I've lost that money". When he turned up with the cheque I was really chuffed. I knew he would, because he wouldn't be where he is now if it hadn't been for us.

'He was the driver I most admired. He didn't have the money, he couldn't afford to do it, but somehow he did it. He bought and sold cars just to scrape a few quid together so he could race. You've got to hand it to the boy — he had nothing.'

Of course Eddie had long since been in a position to repay Firman, but better late than never. Cash was quite a concern for Eddie, and that very day the subject came up again when we stopped for dinner in Oxford on the way home from Birmingham. By sheer chance Eddie Jordan was in the same restaurant with his family, and the two Eddies went off for a discussion of the latest situation.

Irvine found himself in a strange position. His original Jordan deal for Suzuka and Adelaide included an option for 1994, and EJ fully intended to take it up. Eddie was being offered a tempting deal — an F1 drive with no requirement to bring money. But it guaranteed a salary which was just a fraction of what he could make in Japan. His F3000 earning potential in 1994 was greater than ever; the GP outing had promoted him way above the opposition, and with a works Toyota touring car drive with Cerumo thrown in, he'd negotiated a dream package. It was also clear that, longer term, the Japanese scene looked a bit shakey, and 1994 might be the last big earning year. He felt that there would always be time for F1.

'As far as I understood at the time,' says Murayama, 'Eddie believed that he was able to get free from the Jordan contract after, I think, 15 January. He didn't realise that the contract thing was so important when he signed for the two GPs in 1993. He didn't take it that seriously. Obviously Cosmo wanted to keep him, and so did we. We almost agreed on terms like money, expenses and other conditions.'

Most drivers would sell their grandmothers to get into Grand Prix racing, but Eddie had to be convinced that a couple of years down the road, F1 might provide a big pay-off. If he didn't go with Jordan now, the chance might never come again. Deep down, he realised that.

'He had got a taste of F1, the limelight,' says EJ. 'Any great driver needs to be arrogant, and Eddie doesn't suffer on that side of things! The discussion really revolved around how we could find enough money to keep him alive, to pay him. For sure he'd have to take less money to come to Jordan. My argument was that Japan was something you could always go back to. With F1, if you miss the boat, you're away for ever. You can do F1 for two or three years and not lose anywhere else. It's the one thing you can do and always get respect for. I also made the point that, "short-term Eddie, yes, there is less income, even perhaps in the second year there may be less —

Right *Eddie seemed as surprised as anyone when he found himself in a full-time F1 drive.* (Autosport)

but if you stand by me, and I stand by you, and we work it together, there is vastly more at the end of the rainbow than ever you could get in any other form of motor racing".

'He wouldn't openly want to tell me he believed that, but deep down he had to believe it. I kept on and on about it. I said, "Eddie, think long term for once — you're thinking from day-to-day, and it's not a positive way to go about your racing". And if you think back, it's probably one of the greatest bits of advice that you could have given him.'

When Jordan launched its new Hart-powered 194 in January 1994, only Barrichello had been signed up — the British media were convinced that Martin Brundle would partner the Brazilian. In February, Jordan announced its number two: Eddie Irvine.

'In the end we had to give up Eddie,' recalls Murayama. 'It was very, very unfortunate. Of course, it was a problem with Cosmo. Eddie was an expensive driver, and Cosmo knew that they'd have to spare some more money if we hired Eddie. When they knew Eddie wasn't available, they asked us for a discount.'

Pre-season testing with Jordan went well. At Magny-Cours Eddie had a friendly chat with Senna, and their past differences were forgotten. He went to the first race in Interlagos on 27 March hoping to make a fresh start — but he ended up making headlines for all the wrong reasons.

He had a difficult qualifying session and ended up 16th, albeit only two places and 0.3s slower than local hero Barrichello. In the race he made good progress, and by half distance was chasing Brundle's McLaren for seventh. On lap 34 the McLaren suffered a sudden engine failure, and the lapped Ligier of Eric Bernard slowed suddenly. Eddie swerved in avoidance — at the very moment rookie Jos Verstappen tried to dive down the inside. The Dutchman got on the grass, flipped over Eddie's head, and all four cars ended up off the road.

The live TV transmission missed the incident, but a slow motion replay did not do Eddie any favours, for on first viewing his sudden jink to the left certainly looked strange. The drivers were called to see the stewards, and despite Brundle confirming that his engine failure had caused him to slow, Eddie was judged the culprit. He was fined $10,000 and banned from the next race, the Pacific GP in Aida.

The Jordan team lodged an appeal, which was duly heard at the FIA in Paris on Thursday 7 April. This time Eddie turned up in a suit but, despite being represented by a knowledgeable lawyer in the person of Silverstone commentator Ian Titchmarsh, he came out a loser. In an unprecedented decision, the ban was tripled to include the upcoming San Marino and Monaco GPs.

'That was incredibly unfortunate,' says Jordan. 'I could see no fault to

Irvine whatsoever. I watched it so many times and thought it was a racing accident, and to say that it was pre-meditated was a little bit difficult to accept. To be honest I was staggered, and I couldn't believe it got increased from one race. I believe what happened was to deter people from appealing just for the sake of appealing, and it was unfortunate that it had to be Eddie. I was then suddenly confronted with yet more driver changes, destabilising the situation.'

Jordan took on Aguri Suzuki for the Pacific GP and recalled Andrea de Cesaris for Imola and Monaco. The latter was Barrichello's seventh team-mate in 12 months.

A lesser character than Eddie might have suffered a loss of confidence but he remained buoyant — and the ban had a fortunate side effect for it meant he was safely on the sidelines during the most turbulent and tragic few weeks in GP history.

At the San Marino GP, on the Friday Eddie was watching from the grandstand when Rubens suffered a massive accident at the final chicane. The Brazilian was extremely lucky to escape virtually unharmed, but he was out of action for the weekend. Then on Saturday Roland Ratzenberger,

The 1994 Brazilian GP started well but ended up with another controversial incident. (Formula One Pictures)

125

trying to qualify for his second start with Simtek, had a horrific crash at Villeneuve corner. He became the first man to die in a GP car since Elio de Angelis, eight years earlier.

Eddie and Roland had known each other for eight years. Although not close friends, as fellow members of the gai-jin community in Japan, and former sportscar team-mates, they knew each other inside out and had shared a lot together. Eddie was upset, but on Sunday morning he fulfilled a commitment to Porsche and competed in the Supercup support race, in which he finished an unenthused 15th. The tragic weekend just got worse, for that afternoon saw the death of Ayrton Senna, the greatest driver of the era and the one Eddie still respected most.

Irvine has done too much damage this year and should be properly penalised

Next came Monaco. There Eddie made a one-off appearance as a TV pit lane reporter for America's ESPN. Karl Wendlinger was injured in a practice accident, and for several days his life hung in the balance. Eddie returned to the fold at the Spanish GP, and the sport was in turmoil about safety. Then at the start of the meeting rookie Andrea Montermini — another of Eddie's former F3000 sparring partners — crashed his Simtek heavily during practice, although he escaped relatively lightly.

Eddie's return was a successful one. He was heading for fourth place until he damaged his nose on a kerb, and a pit stop dropped him to sixth. With Barrichello still traumatised from Imola, Eddie had a chance to re-establish himself within the team.

'Rubens has never been better than he was at the time of his accident,' says Jordan commercial manager Ian Phillips. 'His confidence was extremely high, and obviously the accident and what happened subsequently affected him. Eddie came back in Spain, was very fast, and hugely erratic — as ever! I don't think he'd even ridden a bicycle in his time off.'

After Canada, where he spun off, Eddie shot back to Europe for his third attempt at Le Mans. Originally he wasn't scheduled to do the 24 Hours, but after Ratzenberger's death all in the SARD team wanted Eddie back as his replacement. It was an emotionally charged weekend for Eddie and his gai-jin team-mates Jeff Krosnoff and Mauro Martini. Roland's picture and an old helmet were on display in the garage, and his name was on the door of the Toyota, along with the other three.

With the 3.5-litre normally-aspirated cars banned, SARD's old turbo car had a genuine chance of overall victory. Eddie was in brilliant form, buoyed by watching Ireland trounce Italy in the World Cup on Saturday night. At the time Martini was slogging round the track. When they changed places Eddie made sure the intensely patriotic Italian knew the result, wasting a few seconds in the process!

The Japanese car led the race until the last couple of hours, when Krosnoff was stranded by a gearbox failure. He got the car back to the pits, and Eddie drove his heart out to salvage second place by passing Boutsen's works Porsche right at the end.

Back on the F1 trail, the second half of Eddie's season was disappointing. He broke his gearbox in France, had an engine failure on the warm-up lap at Silverstone, and was eliminated in first lap crashes in both Germany and Hungary. The latter incident also took out Barrichello, to the disbelief of the team. Jordan's luck changed at Spa. On a drying track Barrichello was sent out on slicks, and took an opportunistic pole. Eddie, who had to stick with wets, backed it up with a fine fourth, although he had electrical problems in the race.

In Italy Eddie landed himself in trouble once again. He qualified ninth, but made a typically brilliant start and lay fifth at the first chicane. Unfortunately once there, he didn't stop as quickly as he wanted to and ran into Johnny Herbert, who had worked miracles to qualify fourth. The race was red-flagged and Eddie was put to the back.

'Irvine has done far too much damage this year and should finally be properly penalised,' Johnny was quoted as saying. His Lotus team boss Peter Collins added 'his brain has been removed and it's about time his licence was too'.

Eddie, seventh in Portugal, struck back with a superb fourth at the European GP in Jerez, where he came close to ousting Hakkinen for the final podium spot. He then took fifth after another fine wet weather display at his 'home' race in Suzuka, but spun off at the final race in Australia. A season total of six points was satisfactory, but more importantly he had held his own against Barrichello, outqualifying the Brazilian on six of his 13 appearances, and starting in the top 10 nine times.

'We never really talked much about the car,' said Rubens, 'but that's Eddie, and I learned how he was. He was always very quick for a lap.'

After Jerez Eddie had been in close contact with Tyrrell, who were keen to poach him, but by Suzuka Jordan had re-signed him for 1995. The good news was that the team had landed a Peugeot deal, after two years of funding its own Hart engines. The liaison had obvious benefits for a midfield team like Jordan and, expecting a big leap in performance from the car, Eddie worked on himself as well.

'He did have the ability to give up or go to sleep in races where he thought "I'm not going to get anything out of this,"' says Phillips. 'But 90% of the time Eddie had total commitment. One of his biggest problems was

127

Strange days. Eddie drove this Porsche Supercup car after he was banned from the 1994 San Marino GP. (Autosport)

his inability to concentrate. That showed itself through 1994, but during the winter I kept stressing to him that concentration was an integral part of fitness. And if he got himself blindingly fit, he would concentrate. And he did. He worked bloody hard in the winter, and at the start of 1995 he was in great shape, from the moment he sat in the new car for testing. No doubt about it, he was fast, almost everywhere we went.

'When we left the Estoril test, we were as quick as anybody. Williams and I think Benetton stayed for an extra two days, and within that two days they found speed which nobody really knew about until we got to Interlagos. Suddenly it was a struggle. Yet again our car wouldn't go over the bumps, and Williams and Benetton were light years ahead. And Eddie asked me after the first day of practice, "what have we got left in the locker to put onto the car to find the speed — Jordan just don't have the depth".

'He was right. He didn't put it in very diplomatic terms. We'd put everything we had into the car, it came out of the box and was quick, but he felt that we didn't have the depth to sustain a fight during the season and make up the margin. Typically of Eddie, it was a very astute observation, but put in a crude manner.'

Eddie qualified eighth in Brazil, and then did a fine job to line up fourth in Argentina, although both races ended in retirement following engine problems. In Buenos Aires Ferrari President Luca di Montezemolo paid a rare visit to a GP, and by chance he met Eddie when on a tour of the pits. They chatted for a few moments, and Eddie, with his usual lack of ceremony, asked Luca if he could 'do something about the spares prices!'

That weekend I interviewed Montezemolo about the company's lack of interest in Le Mans. We spoke in the Ferrari office behind the pits, with only Jean Alesi for company. When Luca mentioned that a private Ferrari 348 had run in the 24 Hours the year before, I pointed out that it had been eliminated in a shunt with none other than Eddie Irvine — not knowing that their paths had crossed the previous day.

'Ah Irvine? He owns a Ferrari, Irvine. I want to know this guy. You know him?'

Yes.

'I have spoken with him yesterday, but I think he did not understand who I was. That was my feeling. Anyway, no problem. He seems like a *sympatico* guy. I don't know him, but I like the approach. On the circuit, and also outside.'

Eddie, Krosnoff and Martini led Le Mans until the SARD Toyota let them down in the last hour. (Autosport)

At that point, to my eternal regret, I switched off my tape recorder, feeling that we had digressed from the subject. Montezemolo had apparently seen a supercar road test Eddie had done for a French magazine, in which he said none of the cars he tried were a match for his Ferrari. When I explained that Eddie actually owned a 288GTO, rather than a run-of-the-mill Ferrari, Luca's eyes lit up, and he continued to wax lyrical about this strange Irishman who had caught his attention. Changing out of his overalls in the background, Alesi didn't say very much, but when asked, he did concede that Irvine was pretty good.

In the early races Eddie consistently outqualified Rubens, who couldn't come to terms with left foot braking on the Jordan 195. At San Marino he finished eighth after damaging his nose when chopped by Nigel Mansell in what turned out to be the 1992 World Champion's penultimate start before retiring from McLaren. In Spain Eddie had a tidy drive to fifth, in Monaco he crashed out of sixth when a wheel failed, and then in Montreal he followed Barrichello home as Jordan scored a memorable two-three finish in a race notable for high attrition. Finally, Eddie was on the F1 podium.

Next time out at Magny-Cours Rubens finally outqualified Eddie for the first time in 1995, but only close friends knew that the Ulsterman's mind was elsewhere. His grandfather Harry, one of his strongest influences, died that week. Because of the GP Eddie was unable to attend the funeral, but father Ed came out to give him support on race day.

After France, where steering problems restricted him to ninth, mechanical malaise set in, as excellent grid positions went to waste: electrical gremlins on the third lap in Britain, engine trouble in Germany (after running as high as fifth), clutch in Hungary (sixth), a pit fire in Belgium (fourth) and engine again in Italy (sixth). Although to the outside world the Irvine/Jordan marriage still looked rosy, by mid-season, Eddie had begun to look for an alternative home for 1996.

'He was badly let down by the reliability of the car during the season,' says Phillips. 'Reliability was appalling, both from Peugeot's side and Jordan's side, but the car wasn't too bad and, particularly in the first half of the year, he was on good form. But he let it get him down, the failures, the fact that nothing seemed to be happening. He got a bit desperate about it. We didn't turn it around quick enough for him, which was the observation he made in Brazil.'

At this stage, it seemed possible that Eddie would be leaving to join Ligier, having impressed then boss Tom Walkinshaw — no easy matter for a young driver still trying to ditch a 'wild' reputation. Discussions reached an

Right *Concentrating on the job in hand. No-one could fault Eddie's qualifying performances.* (Autosport)

advanced stage, but the drawback was a degree of uncertainty over the team's future plans, and especially its French sponsorship arrangements.

'I said to him, "Eddie, you need one more year at Jordan to learn your craft in F1"', says Phillips. 'But he's a man in a hurry, he's made up his mind what he wants to achieve in a five-year timescale, and through lack of resources we weren't able to move as quickly as he wanted his career to move. That's really what it came down to. We always said, "Eddie, we can't spend money that we haven't got — as always, you're a commercial disaster, you don't bring anything to the team!" But he felt in career terms, he couldn't afford another year with Jordan.'

Should the Ligier talks fail, Eddie had even considered a move to IndyCars, having discussed possible openings with Reynard. But speculation seemed to be ended once and for all when Jordan issued a press release on the Thursday of the Portuguese GP. Barrichello and Irvine would be staying with the team for 1996, thank you very much. In fact, the issue was anything but settled. Eddie still wanted to explore other options, and the Grand Prix world was about to get one of the biggest shocks of recent years.

'I was the one that broached the subject of Irvine wanting to leave with

The Peugeot bigwigs join Eddie and Barrichello for the 1995 launch. A works engine deal promised much. (Formula One Pictures)

Eddie Jordan,' says Walkinshaw, 'and at Estoril I asked about getting him out of his contract. Irvine confirmed to Eddie Jordan that that was true, and he came to terms with the fact that Irvine wanted to walk. After that, things developed quite rapidly. I thought he was quick, and if he was handled properly we could have built on that, and made a winner out of him.' Eddie was keen to join Ligier, but the sticking point was a $4 million buy-out clause in his contract. Phillips explains:

'Eddie came to us and said, "Tom's going to buy me out". Now Tom couldn't afford to buy him out. Tom wanted to make an offer, but it wasn't the contracted figure, and even if it was the contracted figure, we didn't have to accept it. We talked about it and said, "we're not going to let you go under those circumstances".

'Eddie said, "well will you do me one favour — will you just see if there's a possibility of me driving for Ferrari?"'

For some time it had been known that Alesi had been kicked out of the Italian team to make way for Schumacher. But then the F1 paddock — and especially the Ferrari management — had been stunned when Gerhard Berger announced that he was to follow Alesi to Benetton. There followed a mad scramble of drivers only too keen to take over from the Austrian. Team boss Jean Todt knew it would take a very special character to partner Schumacher — well known for demoralising his team-mates — and it would also have to be someone of whom the German would approve. Barrichello, Coulthard, Brundle, Herbert, Larini and Salo were among the names mentioned in the weeks before Estoril, although some were a trifle optimistic in the circumstances. Nobody mentioned Eddie Irvine.

However, Todt had kept an eye on Eddie. Coincidentally Mike Greasley, Irvine's new manager, also had a stable of rally drivers and had dealt with Todt in his Peugeot days, but sadly he'd been sidelined by serious illness and for the time being was not in a position to help. Instead, Eddie approached Todt himself, just to test the water. The key contact Eddie had was Graham Bogle of Philip Morris, Ferrari's main sponsor. Then of course there was Montezemolo, already a fan.

'Eddie wanted a stepping stone to greater things,' says Ian Phillips, 'and always, from Barcelona onwards, had hankered after being a Ferrari driver. He'd had contact casually, and they'd obviously seen what he was doing. In his own mind, and I felt he was absolutely right, he felt that he could mentally cope with the Ferrari situation. He didn't have a problem with it at all.

'Eddie (Jordan) saw Todt at a FOCA meeting on Friday afternoon, and mentioned it to him. Todt said "send him to see me in my hotel room," which he did at 8.30pm on the Friday. He had another meeting there on

Saturday night, where the terms were put to him, and he had until Sunday morning to make up his mind.

'He saw various other people, including Graham Bogle, who had been one of the great supporters of putting him in Jordan in the first place. Graham understood the Ferrari situation, and spelt out that "they will own you 24 hours a day, 365 days a year — are you sure that's what you want?" He gave him a lot of the downsides.

'By Sunday, it was, "well Eddie, that's the package, do you want it?" And he told us on Sunday morning that was what he wanted to do, those were the terms he was prepared to accept. And it all happened in the space of a couple of days.'

Irvine and Jordan flew from Lisbon to England on Sunday night, and then on Monday afternoon went straight out to Switzerland and the office of Henry Peter, Ferrari's lawyer. At noon on Tuesday, the deal was announced.

'I've been involved in many, many hundreds of contracts,' says Jordan. 'And I would have to say that it was the best executed driver's contract I've ever concluded for anyone. It was a stunning contract. I was not his manager, but I was asked by him if I could act and do it. I've known Todt a long time; we'd talked about him coming to join me in the early 1990s, and had a couple of meetings at the factory. He was a gentleman absolutely through and through.

'In Eddie, he saw somebody who had experience, who was quick, who wasn't going to be fazed by the press, by Ferrari, or by Michael Schumacher. Someone who could keep his head up despite there being a clear number one and a clear number two; and be aware that with the volume of money that they were paying Schumacher, the team would revolve around him.'

The deal was also a dream for Eddie Jordan. He'd often brought on young drivers and sold them elsewhere, but the $4m Ferrari payout was his best yet. Some joked that Ferrari would be Jordan's biggest sponsor in 1996, and at the time, it was a pretty accurate observation.

'At that point we were without a major sponsor,' confirms Phillips, 'and there was no sign of one on the horizon at all. It basically took the risk out of the winter. If we hadn't had that money we would have been back to a winter similar to what we had in 1991/2 — no money to do anything. But when Eddie went, the place lost something. Some of it fun, some of it aggro! Things were never quiet when he was around . . .'

Eddie Irvine made his position clear.

'I was frustrated. I'm very impatient and I could see it [the Jordan team] wasn't going anywhere particularly quickly. They are making progress, but everyone else is making progress, so in effect they are not catching up. I don't mind breaking down if I'm leading the race, because at least I'm up

Happy days. Jordan (left) gets his money, Todt gets his man, and Irvine gets the chance of a lifetime with Ferrari. (ICN UK Bureau)

there giving it some. We'd be in the points, but not really in contention.'

Eddie was the centre of attention at the European GP at the Nurburging, just a few days after the announcement. Reaction had generally been positive, but he proceeded to undo much of the good PR work of the past two years when in a press conference he noted, 'I've never met a journalist who knows anything about motor racing'. That didn't go down well.

Despite having a Ferrari contract in his pocket, Eddie did not coast through his final four races for Jordan. He finished sixth in a wet/dry race at the 'Ring, surviving an assault from Herbert's Benetton, and picked up fourth with a typically charging drive at Suzuka. Last time out in Australia the field fell apart, and Eddie lay third, and in a position to snatch second, when the engine failed once more. Still, he finished the year with 10 points, and his qualifying performances had been superb. In 17 races he'd started in the top eight 12 times, and had never been lower than 12th. And he'd outpaced Barrichello by 12:5.

He might not have it so easy with his 1996 team-mate.

• CHAPTER EIGHT •

Who's gonna ride your wild horses?

EDDIE HAD JUMPED in the deep end at Ferrari. Joining the legendary Italian team in any circumstances was a bold step, but going head to head with Michael Schumacher, a double World Champion at Benetton, meant he would really be under pressure.

The German star had obliterated previous team-mates such as Riccardo Patrese, JJ Lehto, Jos Verstappen and latterly Johnny Herbert. The pattern was familiar: Michael did all the testing, the car was fashioned to his distinctive driving style, his team-mates were unable to match his lap times, the team took less interest in what they had to say, and their confidence went on a downward spiral.

Schumacher had an even more inflated position here than usual. Ferrari, which hadn't won a World Championship since 1979, was desperate to be up there with the leaders again and regarded him as a saviour. He was to be the final piece in the jigsaw that Sporting Director Jean Todt had carefully put together as he sought to rebuild the team. It took a massive investment to get the German on board — a reputed $25 million for 1996 — and Ferrari had to get a return.

Although well aware that his role would be to support Michael, Eddie was determined not to be left totally in the cold. Even before the end of the 1995 season he was starting to find his feet in the Ferrari camp, visiting Maranello, and getting to know Todt. Just before the Japan/Adelaide trip, he met up with John Barnard, Director of Research and Development. Now in his second stint with Ferrari, and once again working from a satellite office in Surrey, the Englishman was hard at work on the eagerly awaited 1996 car.

Eddie was impressed with what he heard about the F310, named in recognition of its all-new V10 engine. The existing V12 was a classic, but it created compromises by requiring more fuel and extra drag-inducing cooling. The new engine would put Ferrari on level terms with the opposition.

With the final Jordan races out of the way, Eddie awaited his first opportunity to climb aboard one of the scarlet cars. It came on Thursday 30 November, at the Fiorano test track, a couple of weeks after Michael's first go. With the V10 engine still on the dyno, and reportedly having problems, their first experience was aboard the V12 machines, as piloted by Jean Alesi and Gerhard Berger that season. Eddie immediately impressed by being right on the pace.

'I was a bit worried about having a spin in front of all the people,' he noted, 'but I just took it easy, and to be honest the car was very difficult to spin. The first test was just for me to learn the car and get accustomed to it. It was actually Alesi's car that he got out of in Adelaide and said it was undriveable! The chassis felt very, very good, especially in slow corners. It's not quite as good as the Jordan at high speed, and felt a lot more draggy.'

Eddie loved the singing V12 engine, and was disappointed that he would never get a chance to race it:

'The V12 is amazing. I wish we could keep that, so whenever we think we've got the V10 really good, we take the V12 out. The V12 is in a different league; I've never experienced anything like that. But the V10 will be a better package for winning races'.

Eddie soon found his feet at Ferrari. (Empics)

It didn't take long for Eddie to find out about the V10, for as soon as this was ready for track testing, it was fitted to a suitably modified V12 chassis. At Estoril in mid-December the team had three cars on hand. Both drivers did a lot of mileage, although there were signs of unreliability, and Eddie had a brush with the barrier. Still, Todt seemed happy with his new number two:

'Even if he's not 22, he is a fresh driver. He never had an opportunity to drive for a very top team. He's very brave, he has a strong mind. I think as well, he has the willingness to do well. He needs to be looked after, like everybody. We need a driver who accepts Schumacher's position, but is clear in his mind that he is going to be in a position to compete for something. I think he has the right profile'.

Meanwhile Eddie and Michael were enjoying their new relationship. 'He works very, very methodically,' Eddie noted, 'but so does the team. There's a real order to the way the team works, which is important. I think we've got a good little team, and the whole thing is coming together. Michael coming here has really geed everyone up, and they're really enthusiastic. I'm not there to threaten him or anything, I'm there as his number two. We do get on well, or seem to anyway. I'm out to go as quick as I can; I'd love to be quicker than him, but I don't think it's going to that easy, from what I've seen this week!'

Testing in Estoril and at Fiorano, Eddie had been almost on Schumacher's pace, certainly closer than Herbert had been at Benetton the year before, so the signs were good. Meanwhile, Eddie tried to get closer to Ferrari literally and metaphorically by finding a temporary base in Italy, and starting to learn the language, something which won the respect of his mechanics. An Italian friend let him use his Bologna apartment; Eddie got the bed, while his new landlord made do with the sofa. On one occasion they would lose the key after an evening out, and Eddie climbed several floors up a gas pipe and slipped in through a window! Shades of Innes Ireland and his legendary church steeple climbing in the sixties.

Having lived mostly in the Oxford area during his Jordan years, Eddie spent the winter sorting out his new home in Dalkey, south of Dublin, an exclusive area noted for its high population of celebrities. Since Adelaide 1993 he'd been used to meeting the famous, and in the bars and clubs of Dublin he mixed with the likes of rock star neighbours U2, visiting supermodels and Hollywood megas who used Ireland as a tax haven. While partying on New Year's Eve he even bumped into David Coulthard!

Not far from the sea, the Dalkey house would give him a place to relax and unwind, and play about on his recently acquired jet ski when the

Right *The season began well with a third in Australia.* (Empics)

weather got better. He was also indulging in his new passion for flying heli-copters.

Life at Ferrari would be very different from the laid-back atmosphere chez Jordan, but Eddie would have one ally for sure. He'd long had problems with cockpit comfort and a sore back, and decided that, like other top drivers, he needed a full-time physio. Elder sister Sonia agreed to come to the races, while maintaining her regular practice in Kent, perhaps not realising that her duties would extend to chauffering Eddie round for the whole season!

Traditionally John Barnard delivered his new cars late, having honed and refined them in the wind tunnel for as long as possible. With the F310, he cut things a bit fine. The launch was delayed several times, and it was finally shown to the press on Thursday 15 February, just three weeks to the day before the first practice session at Melbourne, new home of the Australian GP.

In the dying seconds of qualifying Eddie pushed Schumacher down to fourth

The opposition had their own new cars out and running much earlier, and had been getting in valuable mileage at Estoril. This did not go unnoticed by either Eddie or his new team-mate. Since the Ferrari was more of a 'clean sheet of paper' design than other subtly updated cars, they knew that if anything it needed more testing and development than the others. But time was running out.

When Schumacher drove it at Fiorano, the car immediately had prob-lems with its novel carbonfibre gearbox spacer. The team struggled to solve that before the last days of the final winter test at Estoril. Michael managed to get in some miles on 24 February, while Eddie waited endlessly in Italy for a chance to run at Fiorano. There were more gearbox problems, but after much hanging around he briefly got out in the car. Then it was straight off to the airport ('at 140mph on the hard shoulder!'), a night in England, and then a flight to Melbourne via a nostalgic pit stop in Tokyo.

'It hasn't stopped,' he said. 'I've been home about four days since the beginning of January. I've never worked so hard in my damn life. It's been hectic. I must admit it's not been fun at all, and I've had no time to relax at all this year.'

Australia could hardly have gone better for the Ulsterman. Despite the lack of miles, the F310 was unexpectedly competitive, and in the dying seconds of qualifying Eddie pushed Schumacher down to fourth. Admittedly Michael was using the spare, but it was an impressive performance never-theless. A whole string of well-wishers came to see him on the grid, including Bernie Ecclestone, Eddie Jordan and former Ferrari ace John Surtees. Eddie kept in front of his team-mate at both the start and, after Brundle's crash, the re-start. But aware that Schumacher was quicker in race trim, he let him through. Despite being T-boned by a wild Alesi, Eddie picked up third place when brake troubles stopped Schumacher.

'I'm ahead of Michael in the championship,' he joked, 'so maybe we can reverse roles now!'

Michael made a point of being the first to congratulate Eddie in parc ferme, although he admitted later that he didn't realise his team-mate had already been on the podium in Montreal. The champion seemed happy with his new pal:

'He's a great driver, and a very good team-mate. He's one of the best I've had so far. Working together with him is very straightforward. You know where you are. I'm looking forward to working in the same direction together with him. He obviously gives me the greatest push compared with all the other team-mates, but that's what I'm driving for, to push very hard and have a competition going on. With Eddie I have quite a bit of that, and I'm very happy with it.

One man and his boss. Todt maintained his support through the season.
(Empics)

'When he let me past it proved he doesn't have any mental blocks in his head, that he is free, and he looks rather for the team performance than being selfish, as we all should do to be honest. For the team this was a very important result, and I'm very happy for the team and for himself'.

The race proved something of a false dawn for Eddie. His season started to go wrong in Brazil, by which time the team had gone back to the 1995 gearbox in search of reliability. There was no time to go testing at a full-size track, and the team had managed only a few shakedown runs at Fiorano. Meanwhile the British teams had been busy at Silverstone, and made progress. With the season about to settle into a relentless pattern of a race every fortnight, it was going to be tough to catch up.

On Eddie's first flying lap of practice at Interlagos, the car bottomed over a bump, and snapped into a spin. It came to rest looking severely bent after a major impact with the tyre wall. He missed the whole of Friday practice, and then had to use the spare in qualifying, in which he managed 10th, albeit just 0.5s off Schumacher. The race was soaking wet and, troubled by a misfire, Eddie struggled home seventh. All weekend the car handled poorly, even Schumacher saying it was 'so bad you would not believe it'.

Argentina was more satisfactory, and he worked his way up to fifth. Three finishes in three outings looked quite promising. But the car was still plagued with unpredictable handling and an uncooperative clutch which made starts difficult.

At the European GP, things began badly when Eddie — already returning to the pits, his Ferrari misfiring — was out after making contact with Olivier Panis at the chicane. At Imola a fortnight later he pleased the home crowd by finishing fourth, and on the slowing down lap was mobbed by the enthusiastic tifosi. However, in both races Schumacher had been stunning; he was a close second to Villeneuve in Germany, and took pole and another runner-up spot at Imola. And he was comfortably outqualifying Eddie.

Monaco started on a wet track which soon dried out, and Eddie got himself back in the news. After Schumacher threw away his pole with a first lap crash, Eddie hung onto third place with a queue of cars behind him, led by Frentzen until the Sauber driver got impatient and broke his front wing against Eddie's rear wheel. After everyone pitted for slicks Eddie was pushed rudely out of the way by Panis, for the second time in three races. The charging Frenchman went on to win the race in the most unlikely circumstances, while after receiving a push start Eddie spun in the closing laps, and was hit by battling Finns Salo and Hakkinen. All three then travelled across the harbour to the paddock by boat, but only Eddie could see the funny side . . .

If the outcome at Monaco was disappointing, at least Eddie had the chance to make a race of it. The next few months were to bring nothing but frustration. The slump began in Barcelona, where in atrocious conditions he spun off on the second lap. He was in good company — Hill and Berger finished their races in the gravel — but Schumacher showed everyone how to do the job on the way to a superb win. It seemed that Michael might just have an outside shot at the title.

For Montreal the team switched to a new high nose in an effort to solve the car's handling problems, and initially this did seem to improve things. An optimistic Eddie, bouyed by a rare chance to do a proper test in Mugello, qualified two spots behind Michael in fifth. It was his best showing since Australia, but in the race he suffered an unexplained front suspension breakage on only the second lap. Meanwhile Michael had the first of three retirements which put an end to any championship hopes.

TV viewers got used to the sight of Ferrari number two coasting to a halt

---

Michael's luck turned around again, but for Eddie there was a mind-boggling string of transmission related failures. TV viewers became accustomed to the sight of Ferrari number two coasting to a halt with a fountain of oily smoke erupting from the rear. It happened in Magny-Cours (after five laps), Silverstone (five laps again) and Hockenheim (34 laps). All Eddie could do was shrug his shoulders and look forward to the next race. As many had expected, Schumacher was doing all the development mileage, and Eddie didn't get a chance to make any serious input.

The British GP weekend also brought sad news which put his on-track problems into perspective. While at the traditional post-race Jordan party we heard that former Japanese rival and Le Mans team-mate Jeff Krosnoff had had a massive crash in the Toronto IndyCar race, and later that night I confirmed to Eddie that he had not survived. Jeff was perhaps Eddie's closest friend among the drivers, certainly in the gai-jin contingent, and he had stayed with him in Los Angeles a couple of years earlier.

In Germany the car did at least last long enough for Eddie to have a chance to shine, and he ran with an unusually subdued Schumacher when their pit stop schedules allowed. That race was an important landmark; three days later, on 31 July, the team took up its option on Eddie for 1997. He'd been told weeks earlier by Todt that there would be no problem, but still it was comforting to have Montezemolo confirm the news of his continued employment, albeit hidden away at the bottom of Ferrari's regular post-race press release at Hockenheim! The Ferrari President seemed happy enough with Eddie when asked for his initial impressions:

'He's a nice guy, he's quick, he likes Ferrari — that's it! It's been difficult for him for many reasons. First of all, because he was not able to test. The car arrived late and there were not enough spare parts. Another problem is that of course it is not easy to be in the same team with Schumacher. But I'm positive sure, thanks to many different facts, that he'll be much better in the second half of the season. For sure Eddie does not have big experience, because at the end of the day he has just done races with one team, and that's Jordan. But he has good relations with the technicians, and he's improving a lot'.

With his position secure, Eddie could concentrate on trying to better his long-term prospects, but he continued to be frustrated by the car, which made unpredictable, wayward progress around corners never mind which floor, gearbox or suspension package was thrown at it. One man who might understand his problems was his old FF1600 mechanic Puddy, who makes an interesting observation about Eddie's brilliant 1987 season:

'The RF87 was a bit of an understeery car, but what he always used to say was "providing it stays the same, I can drive it". If you try and play around with it and try and cure things it's different every time you get in it. As long as it understeered the same every time, he knew how to drive it . . .'

Eddie's luck in races didn't improve, and the string of smoky stoppages was extended in Hungary (31 laps) and Spa (29 laps). Just before the Belgian race he bought himself a helicopter, so at least he had something to occupy his mind away from the track. Indeed, with little testing to do, he spent his spare time on the beach in Ireland. He joked that his grid position was inversely proportional to his improving prowess on jet skis.

Michael was brilliant wherever he went, and in Belgium he took a totally unexpected win. That gave the beleagured team some heart, and he repeated the feat a fortnight later at Monza when the title-chasing Williams drivers both hit bundles of tyres which marked the chicanes. That and other dramas promoted Eddie to a solid third, until he too clipped the tyres and the steering broke. Later Schumacher made the same mistake, but typically his car continued undamaged. After the endless retirements forced upon him by gearbox dramas, Eddie could only shake his head at the realisation of what he'd thrown away. Instead of consolidating his third place he'd pushed hard in an attempt to keep up with the leaders, and paid the price. Later someone asked Michael if he had any sympathy for Eddie's run of bad luck. The World Champion had his own theory: 'Eddie's so lucky with women that maybe he makes himself less lucky with racing!'

After Monza Eddie did some solid testing at Fiorano, and although he was mainly trying developments for 1997, the mileage did him a lot of good. He was bang on the pace at Estoril, and in qualifying was just 0.126s behind Michael in sixth. Timewise, it was his best performance since Melbourne, and the telemetry showed that a small moment at the chicane had cost him a couple of crucial tenths. It was a graphic illustration of the value of regular testing, and even Eddie himself was surprised at how much sharper he felt.

He spent most of the race battling with Berger for fifth place, and even survived a spin when the Austrian tapped him from behind in a reckless last lap lunge. Eddie got his own back by regaining the position as Gerhard hobbled to the line with broken front suspension. He was even cool enough to wait until Berger was not in a position to block him without making it blatantly obvious.

Eddie is the closest a team-mate has come to me in terms of performance

Just one race remained at Suzuka, and it marked the fourth anniversary of that spectacular F1 debut. Eddie expected a lot, having finished sixth, fifth and fourth here for Jordan, but the Ferrari proved as difficult as ever. He qualified sixth, made a good start, got ahead of pole man Jacques Villeneuve, and sat on Schumacher's tail in the early stages, but dropped back after the first pit stop. Still, he was heading for fourth place until on the 40th lap Berger dived inside at the chicane and booted him out of the race. Eddie would thus finish his first season at Ferrari with just 11 points, while Michael's second place took him to 59 points and third place in the championship.

After the race the outgoing World Champion said: 'Of all my team-mates, Eddie is the one who has come closest to me in terms of performance. I hope that next year our situation will allow him to do more testing and help me with the work, given that our driving styles are not that different'.

Having been attacked by Berger two races running Eddie was furious, but the Austrian got away with a one race suspended ban. Eddie headed back to the pits to see his old sparring partner Damon Hill clinch the title. Hill's move to TWR Arrows for 1997 meant that the Ferrari number two could well be Britain's leading contender next season, unless McLaren gave David Coulthard a winning car. That intriguing possibility hadn't gone unnoticed by the Ulsterman.

Back at Monza, before Hill's future had been secured, the driver market was in unexpected turmoil. Musical chairs theories swept around the paddock, and one even suggested that Marlboro would help to buy Hakkinen — or would it be Coulthard? — into Eddie's Ferrari seat. His 1997 contract signed and sealed, and well aware that Schumacher was happy with the status quo, Eddie laughed off such gossip by starting his own rumour about how much it would take to persuade him to go and lie on the beach.

All that really mattered was that Schumacher's recent success had taken the pressure off the Ferrari team, and Todt, the man who counted, was fully behind Eddie. Despite his stern image the little Frenchman is an amusing fellow, and he appreciated Eddie's humour and honesty. They became quite close.

'It's very difficult for him,' said Todt. 'We don't give him enough support during testing, so we cannot expect as much as we might in this situation.

Eddie presses on at Hockenheim. Yet again, the gearbox broke. (Formula One Pictures)

For the moment I think he's a bit lost and we're a bit lost, and we must get back in the game. We don't want to be a one car team, we need to have two. It's frustrating for him, and it's frustrating for us too.'

The boss's sentiments were shared by engineer Gustav Brunner:

'He had bad luck, and it's really our fault because we didn't give him a reliable enough car for a long, long time. He's a good driver, and maybe he lost a little bit of motivation because of that. He's really out of practice. I think he still has a good career in front of him. We just have to make sure we give him a good car. I can see the ambition in him, he wants to do well. It's our fault, really. He looks a lot better than any partner Schumacher ever had, a lot better than the others. He will be the one who comes closest, that's for sure'.

A shared language helped Eddie to relate to Barnard. Although rarely seen at races, the much-maligned English designer soon grew to appreciate Eddie's enquiring mind and sense of humour, and they could compare notes about dealing with the Italian mentality and the inherent communication problems.

In general the pit lane had sympathy for Eddie's position, although the likes of Herbert and Verstappen probably had a quiet chuckle. But the Hakkinen rumours, however fanciful, were a sign that he would have to watch his back. F1 ringmaster Bernie Ecclestone, who plays more of a role as a broker in the driver market than many realise, expected Eddie to give Schumacher a much harder time:

'I've been a bit disappointed with him since he's been at Ferrari. In fact I opened my big mouth at one stage and told the president of Ferrari that at some races he'd be quicker than Schumacher. I didn't think for one minute that he's a better driver, I just thought that at some circuits he'd be quicker.'

But didn't Eddie add something to the show?

'Not really, because you don't see much about him do you? He's not highly visible. If he gave somebody a whack I suppose it would be in the press. If he starts winning it's a different thing. If the guy's getting some recognition because of his ability, and he happens on top of that to be a character, like James Hunt, it's a plus.'

Tom Walkinshaw's view was typical:

'I'm sure he's getting a lot of money where he's at. I don't know that he's getting a lot else. It's difficult to assess his performance this year, because you don't really know what's gone on with Ferrari. Time will tell. If he's going to be a GP winner he's got to pick up his act a lot from what he's doing now, but he probably knows that.'

Still, close friends continued to have faith.

'I'm disappointed as I'm sure he is,' says Ian Phillips, 'because I think he's capable of doing better than he has. I think what is probably fairly significant is that he did some testing before Melbourne, and did a good job, he then didn't test again until before Canada, when he was on Michael's pace all the time. When he's been allowed to have proper preparation in terms of testing, he's gone well at the races.

'Obviously the reliability factor has been horrendous, and there hasn't been enough done to give him equal equipment. I think he understands that, and he's become a good team player from that point of view. He's kept his mouth shut when it would have been very easy for him to slag them off a bit, because obviously he's immensely frustrated. But he can see a future there, and I think that *he* thinks he can still give Michael a run for his money. His confidence in his own ability has not been diminished.

'He's faced with a scenario that I don't think anybody would have antici-

Eddie with his jet-ski near his home in Ireland. He had lots of free time during the 1996 season. (Pan Images)

pated would have been so bad from a reliability point of view. I think what it has done is make him appreciate what Jordan was able to do on so little money with so few people. It would have never fitted his ambition, but there would have been more of an understanding about what we were doing'.

Villeneuve, another driver who started the season in a totally fresh situation, thinks Eddie has acquitted himself quite reasonably in 1996:

'I think being number two to Michael wouldn't be easy for anyone. Eddie has done a pretty good job most of the time, especially if you look at the first race, and again later on. There was a small gap in the middle of the season but it seemed like Ferrari had so many problems that it's impossible to judge from the outside, not knowing what's going on inside. If you look at what happened at Benetton, Eddie is closer to Michael than the other drivers were there. I don't think he's doing a bad job, although it must be frustrating. But he knew that when he signed the contract'.

Eddie Jordan has some sympathy for his former driver.

'I think anybody who looks at Grand Prix racing knows clearly what Eddie's getting and what Michael's getting. I don't think you have to be Einstein to see what's happening. But Eddie's very clear in his mind. He's

149

Captain Irvine ready for take-off. Eddie, now a qualified helicopter pilot, refines his skills. He bought his own machine in August 1996. (Pan Images)

not bitter, because he knew what he was getting in to.'

Jordan knows Irvine better than most, and his assessment is intriguing.

'He's not fazed by anything, he's not overawed by situations. If the car is good enough to win the race, he would do it. The good points are his natural ability, and that he's a very intelligent person. But his brain works at such an active pace that he loses concentration, and wanders onto other things. That's a problem in racing, but I also think that's the sign of a hyper intelligent person who perhaps has not had the huge discipline of, if you like, third level education. That would be my only criticism — I don't think he gets bored with it, but his mind can wander half way through the race.

'I think as he's maturing, his racing's getting more solid. Sadly we're not able to see much of that in Ferrari at the moment, but I think what he needs more than anything is a couple of good, solid races under his belt, some reliability, and the chance to get himself together'.

Eddie himself had all but written off his first season.

'I can't wait for this winter. We can take our time and do the job properly. We always said this year was going to be tough. Next year will be better . . .'

Eddie Irvine's racing record

EFDA = European Formula Drivers Association,
FFF = Formula Ford Festival,
JSPC = Japanese Sportscar Championship,
Ch of Brands = Champion of Brands,
NC = not classified, FL = fastest lap, NS = no start, R = retired,
P = pole, DQ = disqualified, C = class.

1983

20 Mar	STP Kirkistown	Crossle 50F	–
20 Mar	Formula Libre Kirkistown	Crossle 50F	–
16 Apr	STP Kirkistown	Crossle 50F	–
16 Apr	Invitation Kirkistown	Crossle 50F	–
25 May	STP Kirkistown	Crossle 50F	–
25 May	Formula Libre Kirkistown	Crossle 50F	–
25 Jun	STP Kirkistown	Crossle 50F	–
25 Jun	Formula Libre Kirkistown	Crossle 50F	–
13 Aug	STP Kirkistown	Crossle 50F	–
13 Aug	Formula Libre Kirkistown	Crossle 50F	6
27 Aug	FF1600 Heat Phoenix Park	Crossle 50F	6
28 Aug	FF1600 Final Phoenix Park	Crossle 50F	11
3 Sep	STP Kirkistown	Crossle 50F	6
3 Sep	Formula Libre Kirkistown	Crossle 50F	–
24 Sep	STP Kirkistown	Crossle 50F	3
24 Sep	Formula Libre Kirkistown	Crossle 50F	–
16 Oct	Irish FFF Heat Mondello Park	Crossle 50F	4

16 Oct	Irish FFF Final Mondello Park	Crossle 50F	5

Note: Unfortunately Kirkistown's 1980s records have long been lost and it's proved impossible to get a clearer picture of Eddie's early races.

1984

31 Mar	STP Kirkistown	Crossle 50F	R
6 May	Motovox Mondello	Crossle 50F	5
12 May	STP Kirkistown	Crossle 50F	5
12 May	EFDA Kirkistown	Crossle 50F	7
8 Jul	Shell Mondello	Mondiale M84S	2/FL
8 Jul	EFDA Mondello	Mondiale M84S	2/P
4 Aug	RAC Hillclimb Craigantlet	Mondiale M84S	1(C)
19 Aug	Irish FFF Heat Mondello Park	Mondiale M84S	3
19 Aug	Irish FFF Final Mondello Park	Mondiale M84S	R
1 Sep	STP Kirkistown	Mondiale M84S	–
16 Sep	EFDA Finals Zandvoort	Mondiale M84S	11
22 Sep	STP Kirkistown	Mondiale M84S	2
28 Oct	Ch of Brands Brands Hatch	Mondiale M84S	7
3 Nov	FFF Heat Brands Hatch	Mondiale M84S	4
4 Nov	FFF Quarter Brands Hatch	Mondiale M84S	3
4 Nov	FFF Semi Brands Hatch	Mondiale M84S	5
4 Nov	FFF Final Brands Hatch	Mondiale M84S	7
11 Nov	Ch of Brands Brands Hatch	Mondiale M84S	1/FL
18 Nov	Ch of Brands Brands Hatch	Mondiale M84S	NS/P
2 Dec	Ch of Brands Brands Hatch	Mondiale M84S	2/FL
29 Dec	Scratch Race Kirkistown	Mondiale M84S	4(1C)
29 Dec	Handicap Kirkistown	Mondiale M84S	3

1985

3 Mar	Esso Silverstone	Mondiale M85S	4
9 Mar	Non Champ Silverstone	Mondiale M85S	4/P/FL
24 Mar	Esso Silverstone	Mondiale M85S	5
4 Apr	Esso Silverstone	Mondiale M85S	3/P
6 May	Esso Silverstone	Mondiale M85S	R
11 May	Esso Silverstone	Mondiale M85S	8
9 Jun	Esso Silverstone	Mondiale M85S	5
23 Jun	Esso Snetterton	Mondiale M85S	8
4 Aug	Esso Cadwell Park	Quest FF85	NS
17 Aug	Esso Oulton Park	Quest FF85	R

26 Aug	RAC Brands Hatch	Quest FF85	R
8 Sep	Shell Mondello Park	Mondiale M84S	5
14 Sep	RAC Castle Combe	Quest FF85	14
15 Sep	Esso Thruxton	Quest FF85	13
26 Oct	FFF Heat Brands Hatch	Mondiale M84S	2/P
27 Oct	FFF Quarter Brands Hatch	Mondiale M84S	7
27 Oct	FFF Semi Brands Hatch	Mondiale M84S	R
3 Nov	BBC FF2000 Brands Hatch	Mondiale M85T	NS
17 Nov	BBC FF2000 Brands Hatch	Mondiale M85T	R
1 Dec	BBC FF2000 Brands Hatch	Mondiale M85T	15

Esso FF1600: 10th, 44pts.

1986

3 Apr	STP Heat Kirkistown	Mondiale M84S	1
3 Apr	STP Final Kirkistown	Mondiale M84S	R
27 Apr	RAC Brands Hatch	Van Diemen RF85	R/FL
26 May	RAC Thruxton	Van Diemen RF85	4
8 Jun	Esso Silverstone	Van Diemen RF85	R
22 Jun	RAC Cadwell Park	Van Diemen RF85	3
12 Jul	RAC Brands Hatch	Van Diemen RF85	7
10 Aug	RAC Snetterton	Van Diemen RF85	6
6 Sep	Esso Silverstone	Van Diemen RF85	6
21 Sep	RAC Oulton Park	Van Diemen RF85	R
25 Oct	FFF Heat Brands Hatch	Van Diemen RF86	7
26 Oct	FFF Quarter Brands Hatch	Van Diemen RF86	7
26 Oct	FFF Semi Brands Hatch	Van Diemen RF86	8
26 Oct	FFF Final Brands Hatch	Van Diemen RF86	8
16 Nov	BBC FF2000 Brands Hatch	Talon SF86	R
23 Nov	BBC FF2000 Brands Hatch	Talon SF86	R
30 Nov	BBC FF2000 Brands Hatch	Talon SF86	6

1987

29 Mar	Esso Thruxton	Van Diemen RF87	DQ
5 Apr	RAC Mallory Park	Van Diemen RF87	R/P
12 Apr	Esso Thruxton	Van Diemen RF87	R/P
17 Apr	RAC Oulton Park	Van Diemen RF87	1/P/FL
20 Apr	Esso Silverstone	Van Diemen RF87	1
20 Apr	RAC Silverstone	Van Diemen RF87	1/P
4 May	Esso Silverstone	Van Diemen RF87	3/P

9 May	Esso Silverstone	Van Diemen RF87	1/P
25 May	RAC Thruxton	Van Diemen RF87	1/P
7 Jun	Esso Silverstone	Van Diemen RF87	1
7 Jun	RAC Silverstone	Van Diemen RF87	1
14 Jun	RAC Cadwell Park	Van Diemen RF87	NS
5 Jul	Esso Donington Park	Van Diemen RF87	1/P/FL
25 Jul	RAC Brands Hatch	Van Diemen RF87	1/P
2 Aug	Esso Cadwell Park	Van Diemen RF87	2
2 Aug	RAC Snetterton	Van Diemen RF87	7/P
15 Aug	Esso Oulton Park	Van Diemen RF87	R/P
16 Aug	RAC Donington Park	Van Diemen RF87	1/P
23 Aug	Non Champ Brands Hatch	Van Diemen RF87	1/FL
29 Aug	Non Champ Kirkistown	Van Diemen RF87	1/P/FL
31 Aug	Esso Silverstone	Van Diemen RF87	1
6 Sep	Esso Silverstone	Van Diemen RF87	R
13 Sep	RAC Donington Park	Van Diemen RF87	2/P/FL
20 Sep	Esso Donington Park	Van Diemen RF87	1
27 Sep	RAC Brands Hatch	Van Diemen RF87	1/P
3 Oct	Esso Silverstone	Van Diemen RF87	4
3 Oct	Esso Silverstone	Van Diemen RF87	6
18 Oct	RAC Thruxton	Van Diemen RF87	1/P
31 Oct	FFF Heat Brands Hatch	Van Diemen RF87	1/P/FL
1 Nov	FFF Quarter Brands Hatch	Van Diemen RF87	1
1 Nov	FFF Semi Brands Hatch	Van Diemen RF87	1
1 Nov	FFF Final Brands Hatch	Van Diemen RF87	1
16 Nov	BBC FF2000 Brands Hatch	Van Diemen RF87	1/P
22 Nov	BBC FF2000 Brands Hatch	Van Diemen RF87	1/P/FL
29 Nov	BBC FF2000 Brands Hatch	Van Diemen RF87	2/FL
13 Dec	BBC FF2000 Brands Hatch	Van Diemen RF87	DQ/FL

RAC FF1600: 1, Eddie Irvine, 160pts; 2nd, Tomas Mezera, 94;
3rd, Alain Menu and Antonio Simoes, 77.
Esso FF1600: 1st, Eddie Irvine, 165; 2nd Alain Menu, 154;
3rd, Antonio Simoes, 107.5.
BBC Grandstand FF2000: 1st, Jonathan Bancroft, 28; 2nd, Eddie Irvine, 24;
3rd, Julian Westwood, 22.

1988

13 Mar	F3 Thruxton	Ralt-Alfa RT32	4
27 Mar	F3 Silverstone	Ralt-Alfa RT32	2
2 Apr	F3 Thruxton	Ralt-Alfa RT32	11
17 Apr	F3 Brands Hatch	Ralt-Alfa RT32	16

24 Apr	F3 Donington Park	Ralt-Alfa RT32	3/P
2 May	F3 Silverstone	Ralt-Alfa RT32	6
22 May	F3 Brands Hatch	Ralt-Alfa RT32	2
30 May	F3 Thruxton	Ralt-Alfa RT32	7
5 Jun	F3 Silverstone	Ralt-Alfa RT32	2
3 Jul	F3 Donington Park	Ralt-Alfa RT32	2
10 Jul	F3 Silverstone	Ralt-Alfa RT32	4
31 Jul	F3 Snetterton	Ralt-Alfa RT32	R
20 Aug	F3 Oulton Park	Ralt-Alfa RT32	4
29 Aug	F3 Silverstone	Ralt-Alfa RT32	3
4 Sep	F3 Brands Hatch	Ralt-Alfa RT32	6
17 Sep	F3 Spa	Ralt-Alfa RT32	3
25 Sep	F3 Thruxton	Ralt-Alfa RT32	R
2 Oct	F3 Silverstone	Ralt-Alfa RT32	2
9 Oct	Cellnet Brands Hatch	Ralt-Alfa RT32	R/FL
27 Nov	GP Heat 1 Macau	Ralt-Alfa RT32	1/P/FL
27 Nov	GP Heat 2 Macau	Ralt-Alfa RT32	R

British F3: 1st, JJ Lehto, 113pts; 2nd, Gary Brabham, 81pts;
3rd, Damon Hill, 57; 4th, Martin Donnelly, 54; 5th, Eddie Irvine, 53.

1989

9 Apr	F3000 Silverstone	Reynard-Mugen 89D	NS
30 Apr	F3000 Vallelunga	Reynard-Mugen 89D	R
15 May	F3000 Pau	Reynard-Mugen 89D	DQ
5 Jun	F3000 Jerez	Reynard-Mugen 89D	R
23 Jul	F3000 Enna	Reynard-Mugen 89D	3
20 Aug	F3000 Brands Hatch	Reynard-Mugen 89D	R
28 Aug	F3000 Birmingham	Reynard-Mugen 89D	6
16 Sep	F3000 Spa	Reynard-Mugen 89D	9
24 Sep	F3000 Le Mans	Reynard-Mugen 89D	4
22 Oct	F3000 Dijon	Reynard-Mugen 89D	4
26 Nov	GP Heat 1 Macau	Ralt-Mugen RT33	*R

FIA F3000: 1st, Jean Alesi, 39; 2nd Erik Comas, 39; 3rd, Eric Bernard, 25;
4, Marco Apicella, 23; 5, Eric van de Poele, 19; 6, Andrea Chiesa, 15;
7, Thomas Danielsson, 14; 8, Martin Donnelly, 13; 9, Eddie Irvine, 11.
*Did not start Heat 2.

1990

22 Apr	F3000 Donington Park	Reynard-Mugen 90D	R

5 May	JSPC Fuji	Porsche 962	*NS
19 May	F3000 Silverstone	Reynard-Mugen 90D	6
4 Jun	F3000 Pau	Reynard-Mugen 90D	R
17 Jun	F3000 Jerez	Reynard-Mugen 90D	NS
24 Jun	F3000 Monza	Reynard-Mugen 90D	2
22 Jul	F3000 Enna	Reynard-Mugen 90D	4
28 Jul	F3000 Hockenheim	Reynard-Mugen 90D	1
19 Aug	F3000 Brands Hatch	Reynard-Mugen 90D	3
27 Aug	F3000 Birmingham	Reynard-Mugen 90D	R
23 Sep	F3000 Le Mans	Reynard-Mugen 90D	3
7 Oct	F3000 Nogaro	Reynard-Mugen 90D	R
25 Nov	GP Heat 1 Macau	Ralt-Mugen RT34	4
25 Nov	GP Heat 2 Macau	Ralt-Mugen RT34	**3
2 Dec	F3 Q Heat Fuji	Ralt-Mugen RT34	7
2 Dec	F3 Final Fuji	Ralt-Mugen RT34	3

FIA F3000: 1, Erik Comas, 51pts; 2, Eric van de Poele, 30;
3, Eddie Irvine, 27.
*With Johnny Herbert and Rickard Rydell. Abandoned due to weather.
**Also third overall.

1991

3 Mar	F3000 Suzuka	Lola-Mugen T90/50	8
24 Mar	F3000 Autopolis	Lola-Mugen T90/50	5
14 Apr	F3000 Fuji	Lola-Mugen T90/50	11
12 May	F3000 Mine	Lola-Mugen T90/50	1
26 May	F3000 Suzuka	Lola-Mugen T90/50	4
28 Jul	F3000 Sugo	Lola-Mugen T90/50	7
11 Aug	F3000 Fuji	Lola-Mugen T90/50	13
29 Sep	F3000 Suzuka	Lola-Mugen T90/50	R
27 Oct	F3000 Fuji	Lola-Mugen T90/50	*NS
17 Nov	F3000 Suzuka	Lola-Mugen T90/50	13
30 Nov	F3000 Fuji	Lola-Mugen T90/50	9

Japanese F3000: 1, Ukyo Katayama, 40pts; 2, Ross Cheever, 27;
3, Volker Weidler, 25; 4, Kazuyoshi Hoshino, 24; 5, Hitoshi Ogawa, 20 ;
6, Akihiko Nakaya, 16; 7, Eddie Irvine, 14.
*Abandoned due to weather.

1992

| 8 Mar | F3000 Suzuka | Lola-Mugen T91/50 | 8 |

12 Apr	F3000 Fuji	Lola-Mugen T92/50	4
4 May	JSPC Fuji	Toyota 92CV	*R
10 May	F3000 Mine	Lola-Mugen T92/50	1/P
23 May	F3000 Suzuka	Lola-Mugen T92/50	R
20–21 Jun	24 Hours Le Mans	Toyota 92CV	*9
19 Jul	F3000 Autopolis	Lola-Mugen T92/50	R/P
26 Jul	JSPC Fuji	Toyota 92CV	*6
2 Aug	F3000 Sugo	Lola-Mugen T92/50	R
16 Aug	F3000 Fuji	Lola-Mugen T92/50	7
6 Sep	F3000 Fuji	Lola-Mugen T92/50	5
27 Sep	F3000 Suzuka	Lola-Mugen T92/50	4
4 Oct	JSPC Fuji	Toyota 92CV	*4
18 Oct	F3000 Fuji	Lola-Mugen T92/50	11
1 Nov	JSPC Mine	Toyota TS010	**4
15 Nov	F3000 Suzuka	Lola-Mugen T92/50	R

Japanese F3000: 1, Mauro Martini, 35pts; 2, Toshio Suzuki, 30; 3, Ross Cheever, 29; 4, Volker Weidler, 26; 5, Naoki Hattori, 21; 6, Takuya Kurosawa, 21; 7, Roland Ratzenberger, 19; 8, Eddie Irvine, 17.
*With Roland Ratzenberger and Eje Elgh.
**With Jacques Villeneuve and Tom Kristensen.

1993

21 Mar	F3000 Suzuka	Lola-Mugen T92/50	3/FL
11 Apr	F3000 Fuji	Lola-Mugen T92/50	3
9 May	F3000 Mine	Lola-Mugen T92/50	R/P
23 May	F3000 Suzuka	Lola-Mugen T92/50	1/P
19–20 Jun	24 Hours Le Mans	Toyota TS010	*4/FL
1 Aug	F3000 Sugo	Lola-Mugen T92/50	15/P/FL
19 Aug	F3000 Fuji	Lola-Mugen T92/50	**NS
5 Sep	F3000 Fuji	Lola-Mugen T92/50	6
26 Sep	F3000 Suzuka	Lola-Mugen T92/50	2
17 Oct	F3000 Fuji	Lola-Mugen T92/50	2/P
24 Oct	Japanese F1 GP Suzuka	Jordan-Hart 193	6
7 Nov	Australian F1 GP Adelaide	Jordan-Hart 193	R
14 Nov	F3000 Suzuka	Lola-Mugen T92/50	4

FIA World Championship: 20th=, 1 point.
Japanese F3000: 1st, Kazuyoshi Hoshino, 32; 2nd, Eddie Irvine, 32; 3rd, Ross Cheever, 31.
*With Toshio Suzuki and Masanori Sekiya.
**Abandoned due to weather.

1994

27 Mar	Brazilian GP Interlagos	Jordan-Hart 194	R

Banned from Pacific, San Marino and Monaco GPs

1 May	Porsche Cup Imola	Porsche 911	15
29 May	Spanish GP Barcelona	Jordan-Hart 194	6
12 Jun	Canadian GP Montreal	Jordan-Hart 194	R
18–19 Jun	24 Hours Le Mans	Toyota 94CV	*2
3 Jul	French GP Magny-Cours	Jordan-Hart 194	R
10 Jul	British GP Silverstone	Jordan-Hart 194	**NS
31 Jul	German GP Hockenheim	Jordan-Hart 194	R
14 Aug	Hungarian GP Hungaroring	Jordan-Hart 194	R
28 Aug	Belgian GP Spa	Jordan-Hart 194	13/R
11 Sep	Italian GP Monza	Jordan-Hart 194	R
25 Sep	Portugese GP Estoril	Jordan-Hart 194	7
16 Oct	European GP Jerez	Jordan-Hart 194	4
6 Nov	Japanese GP Suzuka	Jordan-Hart 194	5
13 Nov	Australian GP Adelaide	Jordan-Hart 194	R

FIA World Championship: 14th=, 6 points.
*With Jeff Krosnoff and Mauro Martini.
**Engine failure on warm-up lap.

1995

26 Mar	Brazilian GP Interlagos	Jordan-Peugeot 195	R
9 Apr	Argentinian GP Buenos Aires	Jordan-Peugeot 195	R
30 Apr	San Marino GP Imola	Jordan-Peugeot 195	8
14 May	Spanish GP Barcelona	Jordan-Peugeot 195	5
28 May	Monaco GP Monte Carlo	Jordan-Peugeot 195	R
11 Jun	Canadian GP Montreal	Jordan-Peugeot 195	3
2 Jul	French GP Magny-Cours	Jordan-Peugeot 195	9
16 Jul	British GP Silverstone	Jordan-Peugeot 195	R
30 Jul	German GP Hockenheim	Jordan-Peugeot 195	9
13 Aug	Hungarian GP Hungaroring	Jordan-Peugeot 195	13/R
27 Aug	Belgian GP Spa	Jordan-Peugeot 195	R
10 Sep	Italian GP Monza	Jordan-Peugeot 195	R
24 Sep	Portugese GP Estoril	Jordan-Peugeot 195	10
1 Oct	European GP Nurburgring	Jordan-Peugeot 195	6
22 Oct	Pacific GP Aida	Jordan-Peugeot 195	11
29 Oct	Japanese GP Suzuka	Jordan-Peugeot 195	4

| 12 Nov | Australian GP Adelaide | Jordan-Peugeot 195 | R |

FIA World Championship: 12th, 10 points.

1996

10 Mar	Australian GP Melbourne	Ferrari F310	3
31 Mar	Brazilian GP Interlagos	Ferrari F310	7
7 Apr	Argentinian GP Buenos Aires	Ferrari F310	5
28 Apr	European GP Nurburgring	Ferrari F310	R
5 May	San Marino GP Imola	Ferrari F310	4
19 May	Monaco GP Monte Carlo	Ferrari F310	7/R
2 Jun	Spanish GP Barcelona	Ferrari F310	R
16 Jun	Canadian GP Montreal	Ferrari F310	R
30 Jun	French GP Magny-Cours	Ferrari F310	R
14 Jul	British GP Silverstone	Ferrari F310	R
28 Jul	German GP Hockenheim	Ferrari F310	R
11 Aug	Hungarian GP Hungaroring	Ferrari F310	R
25 Aug	Belgian GP Spa	Ferrari F310	R
8 Sep	Italian GP Monza	Ferrari F310	R
22 Sep	Portuguese GP Estoril	Ferrari F310	5
13 Oct	Japanese GP Suzuka	Ferrari F310	R

FIA World Championship: 10th, 11 points.